24 HOURS IN ANCIENT CHINA

24 HOURS IN ANCIENT CHINA

A DAY IN THE LIFE OF THE PEOPLE WHO LIVED THERE

DR YIJIE ZHUANG

Michael O'Mara Books Limited

First published in Great Britain in 2020 by
Michael O'Mara Books Limited
9 Lion Yard
Tremadoc Road
London SW4 7NQ

Copyright © Yijie Zhuang 2020

A CIP catalogue record for this book is available
from the British Library.

Papers used by Michael O'Mara Books Limited are natural,
recyclable products made from wood grown in sustainable forests.
The manufacturing processes conform to the environmental
regulations of the country of origin.

ISBN: 978-1-78929-121-6 in hardback print format
ISBN: 978-1-78929-123-0 in ebook format

1 3 5 7 9 10 8 6 4 2

Designed and typeset by Ed Pickford
Cover design and illustrations by Patrick Knowles

Printed and bound by CPI Group (UK) Ltd, Croydon, CR0 4YY

www.mombooks.com

CONTENTS

0   500 miles

0   500 kms

China in AD17

Western States

HUN EMPIRE

Kucha

Dunhuang Prefecture

Yangtze River

Qinling Mountains

MAGADHA KINGDOM

Bay of Bengal

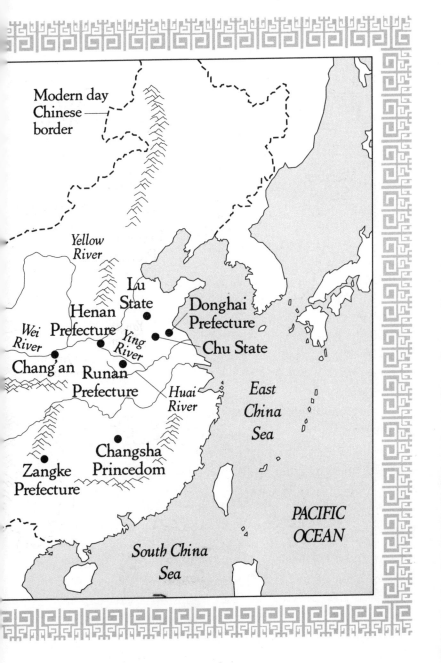

INTRODUCTION

The era of the Western Han is one of the most fascinating periods in all of China's long and colourful history. It is a period of dynamism and change – political, social and technological – an era in which population growth soared, new ideas were explored and society endured wrenching tensions as the old order clashed with new ideas.

The Western Han is the imperial dynasty that has given its name to this era. 'Western' is used to distinguish this dynasty from the later 'Eastern' Han dynasty that followed between AD 25–220. By European dating, the Western Han emperors came to power in 202 BC and their rule endured for centuries thereafter, with the rise of their empire's territory, political stability and economic progress mirroring that of the Roman empire on the other side of the Eurasian landmass.

The dynasty was founded by Liu Bang, an ambitious warlord who overthrew the short-lived Qin dynasty in a savage civil war, but the empire only really started to flourish with the reign of the Emperor Wu (141–87 BC). The early Western Han emperors before Emperor Wu followed the Daoist philosophy of 'governance by doing nothing' – a policy of benign neglect that allowed the population to recover from the economic devastation of war and Qin misgovernment. Emperor Wu changed this policy and used the political capital gained from a series of successful military campaigns to entrench Confucian ideas into government and society, as well as initiating the Han tradition of large-scale infrastructure projects.

This book is set in AD 17, when the effects of Emperor Wu's policies have brought Chinese society to a prolonged economic and cultural apogee. Epitomizing the era is the current emperor Wang Mang, himself a usurper and a reformer in an age that was both vibrant and innovative but also riven with conflict and contradictions. In the book we see some of these social conflicts as they begin to develop (eventually becoming a tidal wave of popular unrest that climaxed in AD 23 when a rebellious mob invaded the imperial palace and killed Wang Mang).

After the fall of Wang Mang the population went into steep decline through war, famine and flooding, and it took centuries to again reach the number of 60 million souls living and working just before Wang Mang's reign in AD 2.

Today, we know a great deal about the Western Han aristocracy through contemporary texts and archaeological research. Palace ruins, the still-standing remnants of city walls and military bases, together with the remains of extravagant imperial mausoleums provide vivid snapshots into the luxurious life of the Han elite. While scholars and scribes wrote extensively about the follies and excesses of their wealthy and pampered masters, their texts have given us very little material with which to establish a clear picture of the lives of the ordinary people who lived in this extraordinary time.

That they were much better off than their forebears from earlier eras is undoubted. Agricultural production increased steadily under the rule of the Western Han. Wheat, together with millets, gradually became the primary crop of the empire, pushing yields to a new height. Ordinary households benefited from the invention of numerous agricultural technologies such as *Daitianfa* (rotational farming), animal-draught ploughing, and the widespread application of improved iron agricultural tools. The Western Han also enjoyed an unprecedented level of craft production, which included lacquer wares, ceramics, bronzes, iron objects, and many other elaborate goods. An increasing proportion of the population was drawn into these burgeoning industries and shared in the wealth that they created.

Economic success had a profound impact on the ideology of the era. From emperor to commoners, the eternality of afterlife became deeply rooted in their minds. While the emperors and elites squandered massive resources to build extravagant mausoleums, wealthy commoners could also build luxurious tombs for themselves. That three of the chapters in this book feature a tomb builder, a tomb robber and a mausoleum minder is a reflection of the importance of death and the afterlife in contemporary Han culture.

Recently, archaeological projects have started to shed light on the forgotten lives of the common people of this era. Among the most remarkable discoveries is the farming compound of Sanyangzhuang buried for centuries beneath layers of mud from the Yellow River floods. There is also the town site recently found in Quxian, with streets, kilns, wells and many other everyday features telling how ordinary people lived. The Laoguanshan Han tomb in Chengdu has yielded some of the earliest medical records and also well-preserved looms, while other finds across the country include numerous mural paintings, bamboo and wooden slips, and ceramic models. These objects bear invaluable witness to the family life, working conditions and deaths of ordinary people of the era, not only in the centre, but also at the frontiers of the empire.

24 Hours in Ancient China brings the everyday ancient Chinese Han citizens vividly to life, combining information from the latest archaeological records and research with traditional historical documents. Where the data permits, the book highlights and dramatizes the social tension between governor and the governed, employer and employee, and wife and husband. We see that even in a time of innovation and plenty, resentment towards a harsh and arbitrary government was combined with a perception that a wealthy few had stolen the benefits of prosperity – a formula that was to lead inexorably to revolution.

As with the other published titles in this series, *24 Hours in Ancient China* offers stories of twenty-four individuals from different professions and positions in society. Compared to ancient Rome, Athens and Egypt, ancient Han is relatively less well known to the western audience. The selected stories aim to give the reader a feel for the rich tapestry of social and economic life while the empire was at its peak.

The stories are mainly based on real tales and actual events in the heartlands of the empire, including the Guanzhong area, where the capital Chang'an was located, the Lower Yellow River and Huai River area, and the Changsha princedom, which were among the most culturally and economically developed regions of the empire. To stitch together the often-fragmentary evidence, the biographies of various people are 'superimposed' onto our protagonists (only the surnames of characters are used), and several stories feature lives on the frontiers of the empire, though these also are linked back to the central regions. By adopting this approach, we can understand the day-to-day life of certain professions or groups represented by each protagonist and realize that, on the frontiers, life was as complicated, civilized and yet ordinary as it was in the imperial heartlands.

Notes on the timekeeping system and measuring units

The Han adopted and further developed the Zhou Dynasty timekeeping system, which divided a 24-hour day into twelve 2-hour periods. They gave each hour a specific name, including midnight (23–01), rooster crows (01–03), daybreak (03–05), sunrise (05–07), mealtime (07–09), before noon (09–11), noon (11–13), sun falls (13–15), evening mealtime (15–17), sunset (17–19), twilight (19–21), and rest time (21–23). Each 2-hour unit was called *shi* and marked by corresponding terrestrial branches as follows: *zi*, *chou*, *yin*, *mao*, *chen*, *si*, *wu*, *wei*, *shen*, *you*, *xu* and *hai*. In this book, we divide each *shi* hour into first and second hours. For instance, 23–24 is called 'the first hour of the *zi* 子 hour'.

Debates on Han measuring systems persist. In this book, mainstream ideas regarding the system are adopted as follows: one *li* mile was roughly equal to 415 m; one *dan* (stone) was roughly equal to 32 kg; one foot was roughly equal to 23 cm.

THE DOCTOR
DISPENSES A
PRESCRIPTION

Guang is about to extinguish the lamp and go to bed when the house reverberates to the sound of someone hammering violently at the door. His wife gets to the door before him, so he hears a panicked voice before he sees who has disturbed them. It is a woman whose face is so desperate he hardly recognizes her as the wife of his great-nephew. She is out of breath and large drops of sweat are rolling down her forehead. In between gasps, the woman informs him that her husband has collapsed, has been in bed since late afternoon, and has now started muttering in a delirium.

Guang prepares to follow his great-nephew's wife out of the door. As he picks up his small lacquer medical box, he feels a rush of relief that, thanks to twenty years of hard-won experience, everything in the box is ready.

Earlier in the evening he had attended a patient suffering from chills and a cold sweat. Guang had prescribed some ground ginger washed down with wine. Then, as soon as he returned home, Guang had written up the patient's symptoms and treatment, and had immediately restocked the pills in his medical box from an iron cauldron that he keeps on a low table by the fire. Sometimes he uses the cauldron to prepare medicines, but when the pot is not in use, it serves as a handy repository for boxes of pills, bunches of herbs, and other medicaments too bulky to be permanently stored in his portable medicine box.

That medical box has seen considerable use since Guang returned to practise medicine in his hometown – in fact it is the second of such boxes, for the first was eventually broken when Guang had fumbled for it during yet another late-night call-out. It occurs to him that his patients often seem to wait for the dead of night before they decide to summon him, but at least they do summon him.

When Guang had first returned to the village, the people had regarded him with suspicion bordering on dislike. Apparently, his predecessors in previous years had been – like many doctors of Guang's acquaintance – pompous windbags who were better at patronizing their patients than curing them. It had taken people time to realize that Guang was different. For a start, he had not become a doctor because of his family and connections, but because he was genuinely interested in medicine. Without anyone to train him in his chosen craft, Guang had attached himself to a series of travelling doctors and had picked up scraps of medical knowledge where and as he could.

Fortunately, his natural talent for the profession had been recognized by an elderly doctor who was entering the last years of his life. The doctor had no heirs interested in entering into the profession, and he was grateful that in Guang he had found someone who would ensure that all his years of experience and valuable knowledge would not die with him. For the next four years Guang had learned all he could from the skilled practitioner, and then after his mentor's death he spent several years travelling, learning more of medicine and herbalism along the way.

In AD 5, the emperor issued a decree calling for herbalists and medicinal practitioners to work at the court. Guang, by now a respected practitioner in his own right, had spent five years at the court and, while there, learned yet more skills from his fellow medicinal practitioners. While he enjoyed working with skilled medics and the prestige of being at the court, Guang had always known that this was not the type of medicine he felt called upon to practise.

Eventually, he had decided to return to his hometown and become established there. It had not been easy to overcome the bad reputation his predecessors had given the medical profession, but Guang had one major advantage over the doctors who had come before him: his patients often got better. In fact he has saved his current patient, his great-nephew, several times before.

The poor lad had been born with a faulty digestive system, Guang reflected. It was a family thing – one reason he became a doctor was because years ago, he had to watch helplessly as his brother and nephew suffered and eventually died from similar chronic stomach problems. Guang really hoped he could continue to save his great-nephew or at least lengthen his life. He did not want to see his brother's only male descendant die childless.

Striding through the village with his great-nephew's wife trotting along beside him, Guang reflects anxiously that he's made this journey too often before. What concerns him is that, despite his best efforts, the patient's health has been slowly deteriorating over the years. However, tonight's emergency is no slow deterioration but a sudden collapse. Guang knows that something must have brought this on, and he rather sharply asks the wife about it.

It turns out that the great-nephew attended a banquet that afternoon. The terrified wife tells Guang that her husband only ate some pork and was fine at the banquet; about an hour after they returned home, though, he started to vomit. Guang ponders this as he strides along.

'When did he have the pork and what did he eat before that?'

'He insisted on fasting last month during the *Hanshi* [Cold Food] festival. He only ate cold food until a few days ago, and then started with solids because he became quite weak after the fasting. He ate too much pork, didn't he? He would not listen to me, and this afternoon he ate too much pork. I tried to stop him.'

The doctor says nothing, since he does not want to worry the wife further, but mentally he curses the Cold Food 'festival' as a senseless ritual that has cost the lives of several of his more elderly and frail patients over the years. All right, so the celebrated Jie Zitui (d. 636 BC) died in a bushfire after refusing to serve the Duke of Jinwen (671–628 BC). Does that mean that other people have to keep dying centuries later? Yet still many Han scrupulously fast from the winter solstice until early spring, eating only cold food, careless of the damage they are doing to their health.

He growls at the wife. 'I've told you and told him many times: the secret to protecting the five organs is to eat regularly, on time and never too much or too little. Fatty meats and wines are to be avoided – they rot your bowels.' Too late Guang remembers to slow his pace and lower his voice – the wife has started wailing.

Early medical evidence

The *Yin* and *Yang* theory closely associated with clinical symptoms and medical diagnosis was well developed during the Han era. Two well-preserved medical texts describing the eleven Yin and Yang blood vessels have been discovered in tomb No. 3 at Mawangdui, one of the most well-known early Western Han aristocrat cemeteries with unparalleled preservation, including the mummified body of the Lady Dai.

Remedies were also described in the texts. Another highly significant discovery at the Laoguanshan cemetery was the finding of many classical canons of the influential medical school of thought founded by Bian Que (d. 310 BC) and a lacquer figurine clearly marked with blood vessels and acupuncture points. These discoveries provide key evidence for understanding the origin of vessel theory and how this was used to diagnose and cure diseases.

'I remember this advice, Great Uncle, but the foolish man never listens to me. You know how stubborn he is and his temper gets shorter and shorter with each illness. My life is a misery!'

To Guang's huge relief they arrive at the patient's home before he has to deal with the panicked woman. Subtly ignoring her sobs, the doctor steps into the house and goes directly to the bedroom, where he finds his patient almost unconscious, shivering under a bedsheet.

Guang goes closer to the bedside, grabs the young man's right wrist and starts to feel for a pulse while he interrogates the wife, cutting her off whenever her replies become too verbose. He establishes that the patient has been suffering from night sweats for the past two nights, but has been sweating even more after he started vomiting. Yet he has not appeared to be thirsty at all, even though when healthy he usually likes to have a mug of water in the evenings.

The doctor nods and moves his fingers from the wrist to feel the blood vessels in the neck, while his other hand gently palpates the chest and back. The wife notes his movements, and informs the doctor that there has been no pain in the back, but she has seen her husband clutch at his abdomen a few times. As she speaks, her husband opens his swollen red-slitted eyes and paws at his belly once more.

The patient's pulse on the carotid artery is normal, whereas his pulse on the radial artery is abnormally slow and erratic. Guang decides that he can rule out an external problem linked to a *Yang*-energy issue. Therefore he is dealing with a *Yin*-energy problem in the internal organs, caused by a deteriorating stomach. The slow pulse, vomit, pain in the belly and lack of thirst all fit into the typical symptoms of *Yang*-energy insufficiency – a diagnosis made even easier by the fact that Guang has seen these symptoms before in this patient.

Fortunately, although his great-nephew has entered into an acute stage of his chronic illness, his face is yellow and not turning black, and his eyes have not turned white. The pork has done considerable damage to the patient's weak stomach, but the condition is still curable. Guang says as much, and a huge sigh of relief from the wife follows his pronouncement.

As the doctor opens his medical box, a few copper needles and *bianshi* stones slip out. The wife gives an audible gasp as she sees these implements, for her husband does not respond well to acupuncture. She knows that the doctor is aware of this and believes that he is resorting to desperate measures.

Guang has indeed unsuccessfully tried acupuncture on his great-nephew on previous occasions, but each time that was

GOLD ACUPUNCTURE
NEEDLES FROM THE
MANCHENG TOMB
OF EMPEROR LIU
CHENG (r. 33–7 BC)

almost by way of an experiment. The problem here is that of internal organs overheating, and Guang is of the school of thought that believes acupuncture is generally contraindicated in such cases. While some doctors of the Qin medical school feel that acupuncture should be used in almost every case, Guang feels that it sometimes merely adds to a patient's stress. He prefers to use drugs and herbal treatment, reserving acupuncture as an ancillary treatment.

With the wife standing over him hopefully, awaiting a prognosis and suggested remedy, Guang reviews his options. The illness has progressed to a tricky stage where pharmaceutical concoctions might cure the condition at the cost of killing the patient. Indeed, so delicate is his patient's health that any strong medicine might be fatal. In the end, Guang takes a pinch of wild ginger, a cinnamon twig and a sprig of the healing herb (*Atractylodes lancea*) and puts them into his small mortar.

Once he has ground the mixture into a powder, Guang scoops it into a small spoon and passes it to the wife with instructions to feed it to the patient. The doctor himself watches to see how well the medicine goes down and the patient's reaction to it.

Seeing that his great-nephew is able to take the preparation without great difficulty, the doctor is reassured that the young man's condition has stabilized. The medicine he most needs now is simply enough time to recover, for once the stomach can accept medicine, the other internal organs thereafter share the benefit. The stomach is crucial, for when it is empty the other organs are drained of strength.

Doctor Chunyu Yi

Chunyu Yi (*c.* 215–140 BC), also known as Canggong, having been head of a state granary before he became a doctor, excelled in pulse-taking and diagnosis as well as prescribing effective medicines for his patients.

The book of *Zhenji* (*Compilation of Diagnoses*), contains twenty-five typical medical cases. In each case, Chunyu Yi recorded the patient's name, gender, occupation, hometown, diagnosis, symptoms, causes of illness, mechanism of medical symptoms (pathogenesis), remedy, cure, and so on.

The twenty-five patients came from different social classes and had different medical problems. Thirteen of the fifteen successfully treated cases were cured by prescribed medicines and four cases were resolved through acupuncture. In ten other cases, though Chunyu Yi gave precise diagnoses, he was not able to cure the patients. Nonetheless, Chunyu Yi truthfully described these 'failed' cases. The *Zhenji* has been praised by later scholars for providing detailed medical cases that offer a clear insight into contemporary medical education and practice.

As Guang repacks his medical box, he commands the wife to keep the patient's stomach supplied with sustaining food, but in very moderate amounts. From years of previous experience with her husband's illness, the wife knows of several suitable foods, and she suggests that on this occasion she might try porridge cooked with rice and a proportion of eight units of liquid to each unit of solids.

Cereal porridge is considered very conducive to healing, for the body derives *qi* energy from the porridge and spreads this to the other internal organs, so Guang agrees, but suggests increasing the liquid proportion from eight to fifteen. He tells the wife to heat the porridge either with firewood or by putting heated stones into the pot to cook it. As the wife bustles about these preparations, Guang takes his leave.

Inside his great-nephew's house the doctor had tried to maintain a professional demeanour while making his diagnosis and preparing to dispense his prescription. Only when he steps out of the building into the chilly night air does he realize that his back is soaked in sweat. Could it be, he wonders, that it is the house itself that is making his great-nephew sick?

Both in his early studies and when working with other medicinal practitioners in the court, Guang learned the popular *shushu* calculations, *fangshu*, and the art of necromancy. In *fangshu* it is believed that many aspects of a house might affect the health of people living within – orientation, building material, the floor and the height of the walls are all factors to be considered.

As Guang walks through the dark streets towards his home, he is mentally reviewing the structure of his great-nephew's house and considering aspects that he might redesign or change. Maybe repairs to the house might also help to repair his patient's health – or maybe not, he thinks, but it is certainly something to consider.

⯜ EIGHTH HOUR OF THE NIGHT

(01.00–02.00: FIRST PART OF *CHOU*)

THE TOMB ROBBER STRIKES OUT

The plateau seems empty in the moonlight, but there is at least one person in the long wild grass, and he is checking carefully to make sure that there are no others. Ji, the tomb robber, is well aware of the fatal consequences should his clandestine tunnel have been discovered, so he has come early to check that the authorities have not prepared an ambush for his little party when they resume work.

Ji is experienced at looting burial sites, but the same cannot be said for the other two members of his gang. He clucks his tongue in irritation as he sees them making their way up the slope towards him. Can't those fools see their way by moonlight? There's a full moon shining brightly overhead, yet his accomplices carry lanterns that signal to everyone for miles around that there is suspicious activity taking place around the old tomb.

It's one thing to be wild and reckless – that's expected of a knight errant, the social class to which Ji belongs. It's another thing to be suicidally stupid. Ji is frequently penniless, and when he has money he thinks of nothing but spending all he has in a single night of gambling, dancing and drinking. That's what knights errant do. They reject standard conventions and despise the dull morality of the working classes. Yet when Ji takes a gamble, he carefully calculates the odds. When he gets into a fight – which is often – he wants to be sure he is going to win it, and for that reason he spends as much time practising martial arts as he does drinking and dancing.

Knights errant

These lawless men formed a new social class during the Han era. They originally represented the spirit of righteousness and enjoyed a high moral reputation among the grass roots of society. But their rejection of convention and a spate of unlawful killings eventually made them a substantial threat to social order and public security.

Guo Jie was a well-known knight errant of the Western Han period. He had a wild youth, being a hatchet man for gangsters and heavily involved in tomb looting and counterfeit coinage. He became more restrained in his mature years and earned a reputation for politeness and for being a capable mediator. However, his children and servants were involved in several murders, causing the Han court to order his execution.

This is why he is now waiting impatiently in the moonlight. Zhu, the older of the other two robbers, had wanted to get started in broad daylight the moment they had located the tomb. He had asked who was going to see them at work, rhetorically throwing his arms wide to indicate the arid semi-wasteland around them. But Ji had merely shaken his head and countered with the story of another robber in their profession who had recently brazenly tunnelled into a state temple. The man and his gang had stolen a fine bronze-head appliqué, but their lack of caution had cost them their own heads in exchange. Thereafter the authorities had gone on to execute the men's families also, by way of emphasizing their extreme displeasure. The robbery of sacred sites is one of those things the authorities are cracking down on, and even the wildest of freebooters is well advised to tread carefully.

It's not as if they do not have the time. Whether Zhu gets his money today or next week, it won't stay in his purse long. A single night of drinking and gambling is usually all it takes before Zhu is broke and looking for his next job. So the two extra nights spent carefully excavating their tunnel under the tomb make no difference one way or the other.

This will be the last night. Within the hour they will be standing within the tomb itself. Ji is still not certain what they will find within. His information is scanty, a mixture of anecdote, rumour and local legend. He knows how these legends get inflated over time, but he really wants to believe the stories that at the other end of their tunnel sleeps the wife of a wealthy king; a man so rich that not just his cabinets, but even his bed was stuffed with gold.

Ji is eager to get started, so when his accomplices arrive he merely glares at the lanterns and gestures brusquely at the tunnel entrance, from which he has already removed the concealing thorn scrubs.

The tunnel is dark and narrow, and the three crawl like ants in a line, Ji first, then Zhu and then the new guy Wan. Ji knows that Wan is nervous about entering a tomb, his head filled with superstitious stories of mummies and bodies floating in their coffins, embalmed in liquids that keep them as fresh as the day they died. Their eyes will be open, and they will stare unblinking at the robbers who violate their repose.

The truth is otherwise. In all the tombs he has robbed, Ji has never encountered the choking gas or mechanical traps of legend. Despite the curses that descend on the heads of those who steal from the dead, he has lost none of his hair or skin. Patiently he had explained to Wan that what they would find would be a coffin, hopefully one as beautifully painted as that in any temple (for this would signify the burial of a person of wealth). Ideally the corpse would wear a jade suit, a stone valued in this life and the next, and beside that would be a jade frog larger than the little box that Wan keeps his clothing in. Perhaps there will be swords, and daggers with precious inlays, or thousands of other wonderful items. You never know with a tomb.

The group reach the place where previously they had stopped digging just before dawn. That was when Ji had swung his pickaxe for the last time while his accomplices cleared the earth aside so that their tunnel did not get blocked. Kneeling in the earth, Ji had placed a hand against the dead end before him and another on one of the side walls, and patted them gently. Nothing from the front, but from the side wall came a dull toneless echo, almost silent, but which to Ji seemed like a roar. 'This must be the entrance,' he had said. 'We will make the breach tomorrow.'

Now their pulses are racing as they hope for their richest payday yet. Wan holds the lantern as Ji clears away the earth with his hands. Ji is rather disturbed to find that the wall revealed by his excavations is of brick. He had been hoping for cypress, a stave wall of cypress timber that would form part of the so-called *huangchang ticou* ('cypress-gathered head') structure used in the tombs of the elite of the Han dynasty. Han royalty believed that cypress was the perfect material with which to build homes for their eternal afterlife – brick suggests the tomb of perhaps a well-off courtier, but not someone buried with the almost limitless wealth they had been hoping for.

In no good temper, Ji knocks a hole in the wall, and then flings out an arm to stop Zhu from climbing in. 'Wait for the bad air to clear.' There's something about tomb air that contains a dark energy, and Ji knows from experience that only when the dank, chilly air has been released from its long confinement will it be safe to enter the tomb. The forced delay seems to take for ever as the warm night air flows past them, yet in reality they wait for barely more than a minute.

Ji goes first, lamp held low to avoid burning anything flammable on the other side of the wall. But when he glimpses the paintings on the ceiling, he holds the torch up high. His criminal career has taken him to many places in the region, and though illiterate, Ji has developed a fascination for the antiquity of the temples and the tombs he visits. Whether worshipping or thieving, he likes to stop and admire the paintings and other artistic objects he comes across.

His conscience never troubles him and he never regrets his chosen career. Yes, he knows full well that tomb looting is very literally a dead-end job. Spiritually, it is a descent into eternal darkness, with no exit and no future. Yet why should such beauty as he now sees before him be reserved only for the dead? Often he recalls a fragment of a lesson he once overheard from a class being held at a busy street market. The teacher had been lecturing on the harmfulness of theft, and one student had quoted from Zhuang Zi, (the Qu qie 'Ransacking Coffers' volume, as Ji later discovered): 'Here is one who steals a belt hook, he is put to death; here is another who steals a state, he becomes a nobleman.'

At first Ji had considered this an amusing and somewhat mischievous quip. Yet the more he thought about it, the more subtle and complex the implications of the quote seemed. Now it has become almost a personal motto that explains and justifies what he does.

Standing in the middle of the space with his torch held high, Ji cranes his neck to examine the paintings. He calls the others to come and look.

'See, these mythological animals show the four cardinal directions. Look, that is the Azure Dragon of the East, the Vermilion Bird of the South, the White Tiger of the West, and the Black Turtle of the North.' He shakes his head in wonder. 'Aren't they stunning?'

The other two look at the ceiling without interest and with obvious impatience. Suddenly Zhu exclaims, 'No! Look at this!' In a corner, numerous coins lie spilled across the floor. Immediately Wan extracts a large bag from his pack, and with his hands an excited Zhu starts shovelling the coins into it. Yet Ji is less enthusiastic. Chewing his lip as he studies the room, he reckons that the coins spilled in such disorder are a bad sign. Funerals are orderly affairs. It is beginning to look as though someone has been in the tomb before them.

A ROYAL TOMB EXCAVATION IN NANCHANG REVEALS WUZHU COINS
(206 BC–AD 25)

The other two don't care. They have found money and give no thought as to why previous robbers might have been so stupid as to leave such booty behind. They have not yet realized what the spilled coins imply. Ji, on the other hand, is suddenly determined to learn the worst. It is time to leave this antechamber and enter the main room of the tomb. That's where the really valuable objects are stored, if there are any to be found. In fact it is now starting to dawn on Zhu and Wan that, apart from the coins, the room in which they are standing is almost bare.

With a jerk of his head Ji indicates a small closed door in the lower half of the wall, which the other two have missed. Wan is new and Zhu has only looted small tombs with him, so they are not familiar with the normal structure of royal tombs. Even Ji has only made such a find occasionally.

With his usual impetuosity Zhu snatches up his pickaxe. He prepares to smash down the door, but Ji catches the pickaxe haft before it can swing down. 'Can't you just for once wait until I tell you to do something?'

Ji pushes lightly on the door, which swings open, causing Zhu to step back and drop his pickaxe. There's a soft creak from the hinges, but otherwise the door opens as easily as if there is someone on the other side inviting the intruders to enter. Wan stands absolutely still behind the other two, and does not make a sound. Ji approves of that, for to his way of thinking fear inspires caution, and even a freebooter should exercise care while within a tomb.

The next room is unexpectedly spacious. After he has stooped and entered, the first thing Ji looks for are the murals. They are of a type he has never seen before. The slightly domed ceiling has been painted to resemble the sky, and a bird in black is outlined against the golden circle of the sun. Beside this are the frog and tree that represent the moon, and other mythological creatures dance around them, brought to life by the flickering flame of the torches. This time the other two don't interrupt, but come to stand quietly beside him. The truth is, they also are rather in shock from what they are seeing, stunned by the beautiful paintings on the ceiling. It is Ji who recovers first.

Chiding the others for their hesitancy, he points out a bronze jar and bowl. They'll take those for a start. Beside the bronzes are two ceramic models. One is of some sort of warehouse, where farmers store food and other things, and the other is a model cooking stove. Wan looks at Ji enquiringly, but Ji shakes his head. The items are worthless, but he gives the warehouse an experimental shake to see if anything valuable is stored inside. Then everyone turns their attention to the coffin.

By now it is clear that the tomb has been robbed before. No one with the resources to have such beautiful murals on the walls would be content with such scanty grave goods in his funeral chamber. Yet the spilled coins in the antechamber give Ji hope. Something must have gone wrong with the previous robbery for the coins to have been abandoned like that. Perhaps also there was no time for the previous robbers to have cracked open the coffin?

The lacquer layer of the wooden coffin has started to peel in some places, but some of the painted geometric patterns and imaginative animals are still visible even in the dim torch light. The red tint covering the lid creates a sense of solemnity.

Ji hesitates for a moment, not because of fear, but out of respect for the deceased. Behind him Zhu is complaining loudly that what they have found so far is little recompense for three nights of fear, hard work and anxiety. His earlier exuberance has been replaced by profound pessimism, and it is with little hope that he watches Ji prise open one end of the coffin with his pickaxe. There is a crunch, for the other corners of the coffin remain briefly sealed. Then the lid pops off and Zhu's worst fears are realized – the coffin is empty.

Ji is slightly confused, wondering why the previous robbers had taken the entire corpse instead of stripping the valuables from it. He can't hide a sneaking sense of relief that they are not going to despoil a corpse after all, but he also feels rather guilty that his colleagues' hopes of instant riches have been crushed. He flaps a hand at Zhu to silence the man, and steps right up to the coffin so that he can see all the way to the bottom. Now he knows that there is no corpse inside, his earlier hesitancy has gone altogether.

Realizing that Ji is probably somewhat annoyed with him, Zhu says nothing more but steps alongside Ji, raising his torch to provide more light. There are a few strips of black cloth on the coffin bottom – strings used to tie the wrapping on the corpse. Zhu and Wan watch intently, their eyes following every movement of Ji's fingers as he explores the coffin floor. Almost in unison they shout, 'jewellery' as Ji picks up a bronze hairpin with bejewelled inlays. Next, Ji quickly finds a tiny piece of gold.

Encouraged, Zhu joins the treasure hunt, with Wan now holding both torches. Yet even with both searching, it quickly becomes evident that there is nothing more to be found. Standing back, Ji carefully wraps the hairpin and the small piece of gold into a cloth from his pocket. He looks around, finding the murals still impressive, but now somehow also threatening. They should go. He can feel the energy of dark *yin* forces gathering in the tomb and knows that they have already stayed too long.

He tells Zhu and Wan to gather the remaining coins from the floor of the antechamber as they depart, and then ducks back into the breach they have made in the brick wall. Still crouching, he looks back at the murals one last time. There's a tree he had not noticed before depicted on the back wall. It is tall and has many branches, all painted with a disturbing reddish hue that makes the tree look slightly surreal.

Ji studies the unpleasant image for a moment, wondering if this was the source of their bad luck. Then he shakes his head and quickly follows the others.

♯ NINTH HOUR OF THE NIGHT
(02.00–03.00: SECOND PART OF *CHOU*)

THE MIDWIFE DELIVERS HER GRANDCHILD

Sons shall be his, on couches lulled to rest,
The little ones, enrobed, with zhang tablets play;
Their infant cries are loud as stern behest;
Their knees the vermeil covers shall display.
As king hereafter one shall be addressed;
The rest, our princes, all the States shall sway

And daughters also to him shall be born.
They shall be placed upon the ground to sleep;
Their playthings tiles, their dress the simplest worn;
Their part alike from good and ill to keep,
And ne'er their parents' hearts to cause to mourn;
To cook the food, and spirit-malt to steep.

Sigan, Xiao Ya (Lesser Court Hymns),
Shi Jing (Classic of Poetry)

Everything seems to have taken place simultaneously in the family recently. They are not bad things at all, but they just keep everybody, especially Tao, fiendishly busy. First, her eldest son's daughter got married, and then the younger son set up home in a house that he had built for the purpose. And now in that newly built house, in the darkest hour of the night, the younger son's wife is about to give birth to their first child.

This child will be part of a baby boom that, unbeknownst to Tao, is sweeping across China. A stable government and an agricultural revolution driven by the twin motors of innovation and sensible administration have contributed to an era of growth that will almost triple the population of the kingdom. It also helps that fewer babies and mothers are dying in childbirth, thanks to improved medical conditions in the Western Han.

Han doctors have developed a sound grasp of the process of human reproduction, from conception through pregnancy, and on through birth and post-natal care. Happily, unless complications occur, most Han mothers see a doctor at most occasionally. Other than baby and the mother herself, the person most involved in a birth is the midwife. Rather fortunately for Tao's daughter-in-law, the best midwife living locally is Tao herself.

As an experienced midwife, Tao has delivered many babies in their village and the neighbouring villages, and in fact she has also delivered her other grandchildren. Yet while she is both skilled and highly competent, she still retains a number of village superstitions. For instance, she almost neurotically insists that the placenta and other body waste from childbirth should be carefully preserved, firmly believing that doing otherwise would affect the health of both newborn and mother.

Early knowledge of pregnancy and birth

The incredible preservation of many medical texts and drawings in the Mawangdui tombs, Changsha City, Hunan, provides a rare glimpse into gynaecological knowledge in the Changsha Princedom of Western Han. The *Taichanshu Book of the Generation of the Foetus* was discovered in tomb No. 3 at Mawangdui. It is one of the earliest monographs on gynaecology in ancient China and around 400 characters on the silk banner provide unambiguous evidence that the Western Han people already had advanced knowledge of obstetrics. They also had some basic understanding of how a child develops in the uterus from month one to month nine.

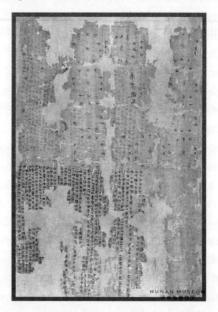

THE *TAICHANSHU* MEDICAL TEXT ON
OBSTETRICS, COPIED ON TO SILK (206 BC–AD 9)

Her younger son made sure that his new home was not too far from his mother's, and this has allowed Tao to keep a close eye on her daughter-in-law, whom she had been expecting to go into labour at any moment. The moment that happened, Tao was ready to spring into action, for the daughter-in-law has a history of miscarriages, and, for all that the current pregnancy has been going smoothly, the midwife is unhappy.

For a start, the baby will be born in May, which Tao regards as inauspicious, for she subscribes to the popular superstition that, as they grow up, May babies have a higher chance of harming either themselves or their parents. No matter that Tao's husband has patiently listed all the children – many delivered by Tao herself – who have been born in May and grown up to be perfectly responsible members of the community; Tao still worries that this baby might be the exception that proves the rule.

The truth is that Tao's fussing about the baby's birth month conceals her deeper worry about the birth itself. Her career as a midwife has been marked by some brutal experiences of mortality, and every time she sees her daughter-in-law she can't help recalling harrowing experiences with mothers during a difficult labour. What if her grandson's birth is one of these, and all her skill cannot save mother or child?

Despite the burst of recent progress, Han society is still permeated with the rituals of previous generations that dictate how weddings, funerals and childbirth should take place. One of these rituals firmly dictates that a pregnant woman should be moved to a side room for the month in which she will give birth.

In wealthy households there are properly pre-planned side rooms for childbirth, while poor families can only afford a temporary thatch-roofed room. In either case, that is where the expectant mother remains, forbidden all contact with her husband, who can only pace about outside and send anxious queries to his wife through intermediaries.

So when her son was building his house, it was only natural that Tao should firmly stipulate that a birthing room be added, with the clear implication that Tao expected her daughter-in-law to make frequent use of the facility. So rigid is the tradition that husband and wife should be separated during childbirth that Tao has seen occasions where, lacking a side room, the husband has been summarily ejected from his own house, or a pregnant woman has been forced to set up in a thatched hut next to a graveyard or in the woods.

Anyway, her son's new house has a small side room, and son and daughter-in-law were carefully coached as to when, where and how they should or should not meet each other before the daughter-in-law took up full-time residence in the room. As a result of his training, when the son heard anguished screams coming from his wife's new accommodation he did not rush to her side, but hurried instead to the side of his mother with news that the birth appeared to be imminent.

So the long-anticipated and dreaded moment is at hand. In one way it is a relief, as Tao is not certain how long she could have kept waiting. She does, though, feel a small flush of professional satisfaction, for so certain was she that the birth would be tonight that she had not bothered to undress, but instead had waited alertly through the night with all her preparations at hand.

As she strides into the birth chamber, Tao checks for the bow and arrows she ordered her son to hang on the wall once her daughter-in-law had passed three months of pregnancy. According to ancient custom, a wooden bow hung to the left of the door to the room will result in the birth of a boy, while a banner hung on the opposite side of the door will produce a girl. Tao firmly believes in this superstition, and the fact that it fails approximately 50 per cent of the time simply reminds the midwife that expectant parents sometimes cannot perform even the simplest rituals correctly.

It is important for Tao that her grandchild be a boy, for not only will a boy carry the family bloodline into another generation, but a male child will exempt the parents from some state duties and grant them tax relief. In her longing for a boy, Tao has coerced her poor daughter-in-law to comply with a series of stringent requirements that have included swallowing live insects, drinking water mixed with powder made from a ground-up dog's penis and her husband's hair, and similarly stimulating beverages.

The desperate mother-to-be has had no choice but to comply with all this because she feels very guilty for not having produced a child after three years of marriage. It is particularly galling for her as Yan, her sister-in-law, has produced two healthy sons without apparent effort – and without the help of her mother-in-law's diabolical concoctions.

The expectant mother is lying on a low bed and moaning loudly when Tao enters the room. The midwife immediately decides that her patient's posture is wrong, and brusquely sits the groaning girl upright before she hurries to rekindle the slowly burning furnace. She has suspected for weeks that this will not be a smooth birth, and she wants hot water ready as soon as possible. She has brought with her an abundant supply of clean cloth and she lays these at the side of the bed along with an ominously large pair of scissors.

It is clear that Tao has arrived in the nick of time. The mother's waters have broken and amniotic fluid has soaked through the thick straw on the bed and is starting to drip slowly from bedside to floor. This will never do – bodily fluids from a childbirth must never touch the floor, where they might be seen by a male member of the family, as this will immediately smite the entire household with bad luck.

Tao quickly averts catastrophe by pulling straw from the other end of the bed and putting it under and around the lower half of her daughter-in-law's body. To an observer it might seem that Tao is rather ignoring the real emergency at hand, but in the Han era it has come to be understood that the separation of body fluid and domestic space does indeed prevent bad luck – especially the sort of bad luck that results from poor hygiene and bacterial contamination. With this in mind, Tao moves some ash from a bucket by the door and spreads it in front of the bed, all the better to absorb any malignant liquids that might contaminate the birthing room.

As Tao is sorting this out, Yan, Tao's older daughter-in-law, arrives and is immediately pressed into service. Tao instructs her to take up a position behind her sister-in-law and hold her around the waist. The patient is actually much closer to giving birth than Tao had first thought – the cervix is dilated and starting to leak blood. How long had the silly girl suffered in silence through the first pangs of childbirth? Hours, by the look of it.

'Yan, grab your sister-in-law's arms and push as hard as you can,' says Tao, then tells the expectant mother to take deep breaths, demonstrating what she wants by huffing loudly herself.

Tao kneels by the bed and puts her hands on the legs of her patient to help her push harder – an effort that is rewarded with an undulating scream of quite remarkable volume. Behind the mother-to-be, Yan looks shocked. It is dawning on her how fortunate she has been with her own relatively easy childbirths. She wants to ask if her sister-in-law is all right, but decides that she will not be able to make herself heard over the din, especially as his wife's screams have panicked the husband waiting outside the birthing room, and his anxiously shouted queries, though muffled by the wall, nevertheless add to the general racket.

In fact Tao is surprised – or more precisely, pleasantly shocked – to discover that, despite the highly audible accompaniment, the birth is actually going extremely well. Miraculously, Tao can already see the head of the baby crowning as it starts to emerge from her daughter-in-law's uterus. The new mother greets her child's imminent arrival into the world with another ear-splitting yowl of pain.

This elicits another round of concerned shouts from the other side of the wall – shouts that suddenly become a lot clearer as Tao unexpectedly gets up and flings the door open wide. Both of the other two women look at Tao, wide-eyed in shock, the younger so startled that for a moment she forgets to scream.

Tao holds up a warning hand to her son as he advances. 'Don't you come in, or even look. I have to open the door to make her uterus open wide and have the baby delivered more easily – but you, stay back!'

Her patient has been turning to get a look at her husband, so Tao hurries back, takes hold of her knees, and leans forward. 'Focus!' she demands. 'And you' – this to Yan, who has been holding the expectant mother up from behind the whole time – 'keep supporting her. This is no time for slacking off.'

Yan, whose forehead and clothing are dripping with sweat, says nothing, but the look she gives her midwife mother-in-law speaks volumes, except that Tao is no longer paying her any attention. Instead, she gazes with relieved astonishment at the tiny baby, almost entirely now pushed from the womb.

Who would have thought it? Less than an hour since she was called from her home, and already she is holding and cleaning a newborn child whose hearty cries signal the possession of very healthy lungs. A birth that she had expected to be prolonged and difficult has in fact gone so swiftly and smoothly that it almost sets a new record for a first-time mother's delivery. Truly the gods are protecting them.

The new mother lies exhausted on the bed, quite unaware that things could have been a great deal worse. She watches with a sort of dull interest as Tao prepares to cut and tie off the umbilical cord. There is still the placenta to be removed, but after the uncomplicated birth, Tao is sure that this will also present no difficulty.

The baby has to be washed, wrapped in clean cloths and presented to the mother, then the placenta will be stored along with the umbilical cord in rice chaff. Some time in the next month, these will be buried once Tao has determined the most auspicious moment to do so and ensure the baby's continued health.

Doubtless the child will cry when she is bathed, and probably the mother will make her usual face when ordered to drink some of the water in which the child has been bathed, but since her regime has led to so satisfactory a conclusion, Tao expects little resistance, even if she does have to explain that the drink helps to protect the mother's system from the shock it has just suffered.

Her son has deduced from the relative silence from the birthing room, the cries of the baby, and Yan's 'Ahs' and cooing, that the birth has been successful. 'Mother!' he bellows, 'tell me, is it a boy or a girl?'

Tao glances reproachfully at the bow and arrows on the wall, but she is too happy and relieved to be seriously concerned about the baby's gender. She shouts back: 'It's a girl. A sweet baby girl!'

Dramatic population rise and fall

According to the census conducted in AD 2, in just several decades (202–130 BC), the Han population almost tripled from around 13 million to 36 million. Even though the population saw a rapid and tragic decline to around 32 million at the end of Emperor Wu's reign due to prolonged military campaigns, it rose again to more than 59 million within less than a century (86 BC–AD 2).

The Stablehand
Prepares to
Complain

The stables are now quiet as Lu walks along, counting his charges and shaking his head at how many stalls are depressingly empty. A gentle breeze ripples through the stable, bearing the sweet scent of the haystacks in the courtyard as Lu stops by the end of the final stable to look out at the broken fence across the yard. It is the third time that thieves have broken the fence this month, and Lu feels bitter resentment – not just because he and his co-workers are going to have to repair it yet again, but because the horse thieves who wrought the destruction have been getting ever more blatant with their robberies, and the authorities do nothing about it.

He sees his shadow cast into the yard by torchlight as his co-worker, Tsao, approaches from behind. Lu is unenthusiastic about flaming torches being carried in a stable packed with flammable material, but he appreciates that his burly colleague had hurried to the stables as soon as he heard the thieves breaking in. Given the chance – albeit small – that Tsao's prompt arrival on the scene might have caught some of the robbers unawares, the torch would have been needed to check every shadow.

'How many did they take?' asks Tsao quietly, and in reply Lu holds up three fingers. He is seething with anger, for two horses were stolen last week on top of the three this time. Lu is wondering whether these thefts are all the work of the same gang, and whether they have paid off the guards to look the other way as they go about their felonious business. Given that stealing state horses is a capital crime, they are either very desperate or very confident. Without corruption somewhere in the ranks of the stable guards, the success of these thefts make no sense.

No one is going to buy a horse of unknown provenance, because the penalties for dealing in stolen horses are almost as severe as for stealing horses in the first place. So, if the thieves try to sell their stolen horses, they will quickly be reported and arrested. No, it is far more likely that the unfortunate animals are at this moment being led to a back-alley butcher shop, and by this time tomorrow the evidence will have been converted into steaks and brisket. Yet if thieves are going to steal horses for meat, why not target the neighbouring stalls where the warhorses are kept? The stock stolen tonight were sacrifice horses, basically skin and bone – and whatever meat remained on their skinny frames was probably tough and stringy. The only explanation for those having been selected had to be that someone had been paid to make it easy for the thieves – otherwise they would have picked a better target. Probably right now some guard was reassuring himself that he had done little wrong in allowing intruders to steal a sacrifice horse, for such horses were doomed anyway.

TERRACOTTA HORSES (206 BC–AD 9)

This is something that Lu hates about his present post. Although it was a promotion, he is now convinced that he should never have taken the job. He has worked with horses for most of his life, he loves horses, and he is constantly distressed by the profligate slaughter of the animals in his care.

Most of his horses are not destined to become cavalry mounts, or to pull ploughs or carts – they are there to die at the altars in the state temple next to the stable, as sacrifices to the gods. Some sacrifices are minor affairs, but with others, such as when the royal family recently visited the temple, the butchery can go on for an entire afternoon.

Lu remembers standing in the sun and watching as horse after horse was slaughtered as a ritual offering to the emperor's ancestors. All that evening smoke from the sacrificial fires had drifted across the stables, and Lu had to set junior stablehands patrolling to watch for fires from sparks and embers still drifting in the wind.

So many horses, all dying so pointlessly, Lu is not particularly religious; he loves his horses more than he loves the gods. While he appreciates the need for an occasional sacrifice, he feels that the numerous and extravagant equine massacres that occur many times a year are a senseless waste of resources in a land that is perennially short of horses.

Perhaps the greatest number of horses are sacrificed not in temples, but to the gods of war in the Han's costly and unending military campaigns. Consider, for example, the failed campaign against the Dayuan in 104 BC, when over 30,000 horses (plus equal numbers of cattle, donkeys and mules) were deployed. Like the soldiers whom they accompanied, few of the animals made it back alive.

To keep up the supply of horses needed for warfare and the ever more demanding transport sector, the government tries to encourage private horse breeders through a variety of incentives, including exemptions from forced labour. Nevertheless, the majority of government horses are kept in government stables – the royal stables of Weiyang, Chenghua, Qima, Luling and Taoyu alone contain at least 10,000 horses apiece, and each prefecture government has its own stables besides. The total number of state-owned horses, at between 300,000 to 400,000, is mind-bogglingly high – beyond Lu's imagining.

Likewise, the number of horses that perish in religious sacrifices almost defies belief. There are thirty-six state stables in Lu's region alone. Multiply that by others across the country and the overall figure for horses sacrificed was huge. Thousands at least! Far too many!

Horse administration

The Han court recognized the importance of cavalry units mounted on thoroughbred steeds for mobile warfare. They introduced substantial breeding stocks from the Huns, Tayuen, Kangju, Wusun and other neighbouring powers through economic, political and cultural exchanges such as *heqin* (marriage) and trade. Once these thoroughbreds arrived, strict laws were introduced to keep the valued breeds within the country. For example, a decree of the Emperor Zhao dictated that no horses taller than 5 ft 9 in could be taken beyond the border.

It makes Lu indignant that someone higher up in authority seems to have reached the conclusion that there is little point in zealously feeding horses that are soon going to die anyway. Lu has noticed that recent deliveries of fodder for the horses are of a much poorer quality than previously. A few days ago he had checked the contents of one of the supply carts, noting with disgust that the supplies were mainly dry grass with hardly any fine fodder such as millet and wheat.

Lu's horses are getting thinner and thinner, and he resolves to comment on this in his regular report to the department, a report in which he also intends to complain about the increasingly frequent horse thefts. In truth, Lu does not expect anything to happen as a result of his efforts, but perhaps his words might eventually be picked up by an official auditor, alerting them to the long and growing catalogue of neglect.

This job is certainly not why Lu became a groom. He and his co-worker Tsao are highly proficient tamers and judges of horses – so much so that horse-keepers from neighbouring parts of the stables often call on their expertise. Lu made his reputation in an earlier job at a stable for warhorses, where his role in selecting thoroughbreds for breeding had dramatically improved the overall quality of the stock.

'The key to examining any horse is to look directly into its eyes,' Lu often said, quoting the principle that his old instructor had taught him. This standard examination includes the size, fullness, lustre and movement of the eyes, and also the outline and shape of the eyelashes and ocular muscles. This, combined with how well the horse coordinates its forelegs and hindquarters when moving, can tell a trained observer whether the creature is in good physical condition and has a good metabolism. In turn, condition and metabolism determine the horse's physical capabilities and running speed.

Frustratingly, the skills of Tsao and Lu are of little use in their current stable. It appears that, with horseflesh, the gods are content with second-best – to put it kindly. Many of the horses in Lu's care show by their coats, their gait and physical dimensions that they are extremely low quality – cast-offs, hacks and screws. Since no one expects Lu and Tsao to train these horses into muscular thoroughbreds, no one can be bothered to give their charges decent fodder either.

A relative of Lu had once incautiously mentioned how the state stables produced such strong, handsome horses. He was rather taken aback by the tirade that Lu launched in reply. 'These days no one breeds anything but cavalry horses properly. For the inferior breeds of horses used for sacrificial offerings and suchlike, do you think the state will waste resources and feed prime fodder to animals that will only be slaughtered for nothing?'

Now, Lu decides that since Tsao is here with a torch, he might as well put the extra light to good use, so he asks his co-worker to accompany him as he walks back between the stalls. For all that they share a common expertise with horses, Lu and Tsao are almost comically different in appearance. Lu is small and thin, with a prematurely aged but highly animated face, while Tsao is a hulking figure, tall and broad-shouldered with flat, expressionless features. When people comment on the difference, Lu remarks that most of his forebears were tall – he himself just has not grown up yet.

The horses in their care are never going to win Best of Breed awards, but nevertheless Lu and his co-worker have developed close ties with the animals over the years. A possible exception to the overall poor quality of the horses in Lu's part of the stable is a little thoroughbred colt. Lu wants to take a closer look at the young animal, which has not been eating properly for the past few days, and had been lying curled up in the front corner of its stall when he passed it on his earlier inspection.

Lu squats and looks straight into the colt's dark eyes. They are big and full, and though the animal is a little frightened by the human looming over him, their lustre is not diminished, even by torchlight. The wide, squarish nose snuffles the air and the small, pointed ears are twitching and alert.

A colt of this quality has no place in Lu's stable, but the stablehands are certainly not going to seek alternative accommodation for their little thoroughbred. Satisfied, Lu points out the colt to his co-worker with a pleased gesture.

'Yes, horses with big eyes run fast, and those with small eyes run slowly. Then why do some horses with big eyes not run?' Tsao is quoting a well-known passage from the *Xiang Ma Jing*, a classic text that is compulsory reading for anyone who wants to call themselves a judge of horseflesh.

'Those with lustrous eyes and swift moves don't run – why? Because their eyes can't see through their eyelashes.' Lu picks a few more passages from the same canon and continues, 'Those

Classic ways of identifying a thoroughbred

The *Xiang Ma Jing* is a lengthy text written on a silk banner that was discovered in tomb No. 3 at the Mawangdui site. The tomb is thought to belong to the second Marquis of Dai, Li Xi. Alongside the *Xiang Ma Jing*, another silk funeral banner, three maps also drawn on silk and hundreds of grave objects were also found. Opinions differ over whether this surviving text represents more or less the whole of the *Xiang Ma Jing* or if a substantial part is still missing. When discovered, the text represented a breakthrough in modern understanding of Han horse-breeding techniques and knowledge.

THE GOLDEN HORSE OF MAOLING, THOUGHT TO HAVE BEEN ONE OF MANY OFFERINGS FOUND IN THE BURIAL PIT OF EMPEROR WU'S SISTER, PRINCESS PINGYANG. IT REPRESENTS ONE OF THE FINER BREEDS OF HORSE IMPORTED BY THE EMPEROR

that could become prime breeding stock, but do not turn out that way – why? Because their living conditions are not suitable.'

This reminds him again of the poor-quality fodder shipment they have just received and it really irritates him. 'What are we doing here Tsao? We're wasted in this position.'

His co-worker is not prepared to answer Lu's embittered question, and temporizes by replying with a different one. 'Do you know that just as we have a classic text for judging horses, there is another for identifying dogs? Ears, chest and torso are the things to look at – but not so much their eyes. I wouldn't mind judging a horse by the ears or chest – I find it a bit sad looking into the trusting eyes of a horse, especially a colt like this, knowing that it's doomed to die as a sacrifice.'

'Yes, but can you imagine keeping dogs in the same conditions as these horses? I have heard that the royal dogs are kept in pens close to the palace in the capital and are well taken care of. Horses and dogs are both animals, but their fates are so different!' Tsao knows when Lu is off on a flight of hyperbole, so for the moment he keeps quiet. In fact both men are well aware that, like horses, many dogs suffer terribly through the unthinking cruelty of the callous humans who are responsible for them.

Now thoroughly annoyed, Lu is mentally rewriting the letter he intends to send to his superiors. Not only is starving his horses unnecessarily cruel, it is also a false economy. Lu intends to forcibly remind the administration of the impact a disease had that spread to the horses in his stable a year ago. The fatalities in his part of the stable were horrendous. So many horses died that an investigation was ordered. Autopsies were performed on some of their carcasses to determine the cause of death, but (for reasons that Lu could guess at all too well), by the time these were eventually authorized, the dead horses had decayed to the point that nothing worth investigating remained.

For a while, Lu and Tsao had worried that they might be made scapegoats for the disproportionate number of deaths. To defend himself, Lu had readied his copies of the reports and complaints he had made about conditions in the stable, but either the investigators were aware of those reports already, or they felt that for the stablehands to see their beloved horses suffer and die was punishment enough, for neither Lu nor Tsao ever heard the results of the investigation.

In fact, the official reaction had reduced Lu almost to tears of hopeless frustration, for once the epidemic had passed, officialdom decided that the answer lay in prayer. Lu and his colleagues had been summoned to the cavalry stables so that everyone could offer up thanks to heaven for the expulsion of diseases and disasters, and to pray that all the horses should grow up strong and sturdy. Lu certainly shares the wishes expressed in those prayers, but he would like to have seen less emphasis on divine aid and more on millet in the rations. At one point the person leading the prayers launched into a specific series of incantations asking that each horse be granted a strong head, ears, eyes, spine, belly and even tail, with every incantation revealing an ever more comprehensive ignorance of horses. As Tsao remarked afterwards, although the prayer was about horses, it was actually a load of bull.

At least the awful epidemic has given Lu some leverage, for he could remind his superiors that if they were stingy with food rations for the stables, his horses would be less able to fight off disease. While the management might be able to pass off one disastrous epidemic as bad luck, a second would certainly cause inconvenient questions to be asked – especially as Lu sometimes suspected that someone was being paid to supply good-quality rations and was profiting from the difference in the price for the barely edible material the horses actually received.

If there was just some way to prove his suspicions, Lu would be able to secure decent food not only for the horses, but also for their carers, for they too – the workers in the stables – habitually failed to receive adequate supplies from the department.

'We are like horses, but even inferior to horses, aren't we?' Lu would occasionally rant to his co-worker, 'Strong soldiers get ill if they lack food to nurture and sustain their bodies, and horses die early if they are not fed properly. What is the difference between them and us?'

Tonight, Tsao is in no mood for Lu's radicalism, so he walks to the back of the stable. The colt's sire is there – the one real thoroughbred kept in their stable. Petting that horse and feeding it little treats is the one thing guaranteed to calm down the excitable Lu, and even though Lu knows he is being manipulated, he cannot help but go along with it.

He stands in front of the thoroughbred, acknowledging to himself that it always gives him an odd feeling to be staring up at the huge head so close to his own, feeling his gaze absorbed by the large, strangely intelligent brown eyes of the horse.

They say that the best horses under heaven often forget their own existence when they are strolling unhurriedly through a verdant meadow, or galloping furiously, like a fierce wind. This horse should be doing one or the other of those things, thinks Lu – such a magnificent animal does not belong here in his sad stable. He absent-mindedly pets the side of the thoroughbred's neck, noting that the creature is unusually placid tonight, perhaps because the stalls on either side of him are now empty.

'Lu, are you going to stand there all night like a moonstruck calf?' enquires Tsao. 'Why don't you go back to your rooms and get some rest – especially since you have an early start tomorrow? I will stay and feed some hay to the horses.'

THE HOUSEWIFE AT THE FLOUR MILL

T he dawn has barely lightened the sky when three generations of the Zhu family rise to begin their day much earlier than usual. Lan, her mother-in-law and Lan's daughter all have a common purpose in being among the first to wake in their neighbourhood. It is early May – that lean time of the year when the family are usually getting to the bottom of their last storage vat of grain.

Yet this year the womenfolk have a pleasant problem; first, last year's harvest was particularly abundant, so there are still several untouched vats of grain in the storage room. And second, the winter wheat harvest has come in early. For once the family actually has more grain than they can store, so for the past few days the three women – or as Lan insists, two women and a girl – have been getting up early to turn last year's grain into flour and to make room in the vats for the winter harvest.

Lan does not need to be told that the Zhu family and others in their neighbourhood are really fortunate in their self-sufficiency. Some parts of the country have been hit by natural disasters, and in others poor farming techniques have resulted in reduced yields or even total crop failure. In such places the price of grain has skyrocketed, despite the government's attempts to distribute food from state granaries to those in the affected areas. Welcome as the grain has been, it is inadequate compared to the scale of the disaster. Famine victims have bitterly derided those out-of-touch officials who have suggested that they should boil wood for food – a stupidly optimistic idea that has been given an equally ridiculous name, *mu lao* (wood cheese).

Of all the Zhu family, Lan's mother-in-law best understands what is happening elsewhere, for her bitter childhood memories of famine haunt her to this day. Before local farmers started growing winter wheat, they were dependent on millet, and their food reserves would often run out towards the end of May.

The planting of winter wheat has radically changed the situation, and these days farmers can replenish their storage vats with a second harvest just at that critical time at the end of spring when their storage vats become empty. It took time to adjust to the new crop, for initially the farmers tried to dehusk the wheat using the tried-and-trusted technique of pounding the grain with pestle and mortar. The pounded grains were then boiled and made into a kind of whole-grain porridge that still contained a great deal of wheat-chaff waste. The result was food so poor that it was considered fit to be eaten only by savages and poor farmers. Lan's mother-in-law will often ramble on about her memories of such unpleasant meals while her granddaughter pretends to listen.

Shivering slightly in the grey light of early dawn, the three women walk into the yard to work at the stone rotary mill – a device that has greatly changed their lives. Any peasants who ask what the government has ever done for them will have to admit that the stone rotary mill is a good part of the answer. The mill was developed first in the Han court, and once it was discovered that these devices could grind wheat grain into fine flour, the government realized that they had – very literally – a revolutionary technology on their hands. Technicians were sent out across the country to instruct people in how to make and use the mills, and within a decade wheat went from being the main ingredient in crude porridge to being baked into bread, noodles and fancy cakes.

A CLAY POTTERY MODEL SHOWING A FARMER WORKING A TILT-HAMMER
GRAIN POUNDER NEXT TO A ROTARY MILL, SECOND CENTURY AD

The Zhu family have installed their mill in the middle of the yard under a crude shelter. Every time the grandmother passes, she touches one of the millstones that has so changed her life, 'Whoever invented this should be worshipped in a temple,' she says. And then she reminds Lan, 'When I die, bury one of these with me.'

Beside the mill sits a large mortar, though even this design has been improved since the grandmother first used one as a girl. The mortar is basically a large stone basin with a base loosely set into the ground. At the top of the basin is an 'L'-shaped wooden rod attached to a bench by a lever.

The Zhu family's three women work as a well-organized team. Lan's daughter Mei goes to the mortar to start the morning's work by pumping the stick so that the short arm of the 'L'-shaped wooden rod pounds the wheat and cracks the hard shell of the grain. The broken kernels are then passed to Lan, who carries a large sieve with which to separate the wheat from the chaff. She does this by putting into the sieve the crushed grains that her daughter has given her and carefully tossing the contents into the air. The heavier kernels fall back into the sieve, while the lighter chaff is carried off by the breeze created by the tossing movement that launched them into the morning air.

Once Lan has winnowed and partially dehusked the grains, she will take her work for her mother-in-law to pour between the grindstones as she turns the mill. The mill is not large, and

Cakes and bread

The Han document, *Jijiupian*, a first-century BC primer and a proto-dictionary, describes wheat as the 'food of barbarians and farmers'. The diet of the aristocracy was different. Some nobles had a '*Tangguan* officer' responsible for processing fine flour from rice, millet or wheat. However, as numerous archaeological finds of stone mills testify, fine-flour processing equipment was not restricted to the elite. Wheat became increasingly dominant in flour production. Together, wheat farming, wheat-flour processing and wheat-based foods revolutionized the diet of those living in the Han period.

Lan could do everything herself, but the grandmother insists on helping. In the past, Lan has repeatedly told her mother-in-law, 'Mother, you should rest inside or just supervise.'

Her suggestion falls on deaf ears, for not only is the grandmother the most stubborn person in the family, but even after all these years she still takes a simple delight in turning the mill and making fine, useful flour from the formerly despised wheat.

This morning, Lan observes that their domestic production line has hit a snag at the very first stage, on the bench of the mortar. Here the heavy pounding of yesterday has knocked the wooden stick out of alignment. Mei pumps the rod up and down but she is only pounding the edge of the basin, leaving the grains in the middle untouched.

The girl tries to drag the skewed wooden rod back to its proper position, but Lan knows that the mechanism will not work until it is fixed properly by her husband. She tells her daughter that rather than wasting time with the rod, she should use the hand quern instead. The daughter obeys, scowling. Lan knows that this is partly because her child resents having to whack at the wheat with the quern as if she were some crude northern barbarian, but also because the quern is heavy (about 5 kg) and Mei has to lift it high if she is properly to crack the grains.

Lan sighs, knowing that everyone will be slowed down, the quern being much less efficient. With the rod-and-lever mechanism the daughter can crush two full handfuls of grain at once (around half a kilogram); now she will have to work hard to maintain a fraction of that pace.

Mei will tire fast from pounding with the quern, so Lan – as she cleans the floor and fits a mesh to the winnowing basket – keeps an eye on her daughter. As Mei finishes dehusking the first batch of grain, Lan rolls the heavy mortar on the floor just a tiny bit closer to the basket and holds it tilted so that her daughter can use both her hands to move the pounded grain into the mesh.

It is time for Mei to practise winnowing, so Lan passes the basket to her daughter and watches closely, because the girl has not had a lot of practice at this. The daughter knows to keep her arms wide open, embracing the sieve, while her legs are together and her feet turned out. Then, all she needs to do is to toss the grain from the mesh held in place between her arms and legs. Executing this manoeuvre perfectly is much easier in theory than in practice, and getting it right does indeed require a lot of practice.

The daughter's upper arms are strong, but her legs and forearms are not. She shakes the mesh strenuously and tries to keep her legs steady. After a minute of vigorous shaking, most of the chaff fragments remain in the mesh, and half of the sieved grains have fallen outside the sieve onto the packed clay of the courtyard.

This causes general delight among chickens gathered there; they flock to enjoy a fine breakfast of partially processed food grains. Every morning that the family grind flour is a feast for the birds that patrol the yard, pecking at the chaff and other leftovers from the grain processing. Now they crowd around the daughter, clucking and squawking as they squabble over the bounty that has spilled from the mesh. This is too much for the grandmother, who rushes over with shrill curses, kicking at any chickens not fast enough to get out of her way. The habits of a hungry childhood are too deeply ingrained in the old woman for her to see a single handful of spring grain go to waste.

Lan sweeps up some of the dehusked grains and quickly and adroitly re-sieves them, twisting her wrists so that the dirt from the courtyard drops back through the mesh. She remembers when she was a teenager struggling to operate the unwieldy sieve, so she gives her child a consoling pat on the shoulder before she walks to the stone mill to grind the first load.

The mill is turned with a bar fitted through its upper part, and Lan walks in a slow circle as she pushes the bar around the mill. As she does so, the grandmother scoops grain from the basket and adds it to the mill through a groove on the top. As the grain is slowly added they can hear the crackling sound of the granite mill stones pulverizing the kernels. That sound fades away after Lan rotates the mill for a few laps, feeling the pressure against the bar getting lighter as the grain turns to powder. Once she meets little resistance, Lan stops pushing, and everyone helps to lift off the upper part of the stone mill and rest it upside down on the floor. The grandmother sweeps up the crushed grain from the grooves in the lower part of the stone mill and also from the surface of both the lower and upper parts, catching the flour in a fine mesh made of bamboo.

Mei watches her mother pick up a sieve. 'Why are we sieving the flour again?' she asks, observing that the flour has already been ground to the quality needed to make fine bread. Lan explains that tomorrow the family are offering the first fruits of the harvest to their ancestors, and the cakes and buns they will give must be the finest they can prepare.

In any case, one sieving is seldom enough. Lan remembers that some of the first stone mills in her region had shaped grooves radiating from the middle to the edge of the grindstone, and it was normal that half-ground grain would get trapped in these large grooves. The Zhu family's mill is an improved design, in which the radial lines of the grooves are now cut across each other to create finer grooves. This has not entirely solved the problem, however, so flour, to be properly refined, needs to be ground and sieved several times before all the husks, chaff, dirt and grit are gone from the final product.

Lan has a broken tooth to remind her that sand particles can turn up unexpectedly in food made from poorly sieved wheat flour. Her mother-in-law avoids this issue by having few teeth at all. Although Lan is keeping the idea to herself, she wants some of the extra-fine flour to make softer bread for the old lady. Lan has been secretly learning from some other women in the village a new technique of fermentation, which makes bread softer and much easier to chew. 'So many new ideas these days,' she marvels to herself. She knows that her mother-in-law will object to the extra time and ingredients needed for her special bread, so while they are working on the offering cakes, she plans to quietly prepare the new bread, and give it to her mother-in-law unasked.

The daughter has noticed another issue – the ritual is to offer thanks for this year's plentiful harvest, yet this morning they are grinding wheat from last year's crop. Shouldn't this year's harvest be celebrated with this year's grain?

'That is right.' The grandmother nods her head in approval. 'We ought to do that! But we also should always honour our ancestors with our best yield from the land. The new grain is not available just yet – there was too much rain while they were harvesting and now the grain has to dry. Tomorrow we will boil the new grains and offer some to our ancestors in our finest bowl. To compensate for the boiled grain, we will grind this flour as finely as possible and make a cake, which we will decorate as elegantly as we can.'

Lan is standing under the roof of the corridor, sieving the flour one last time when she spots another problem. She calls over her mother-in-law with a worried frown on her face. On the fine-mesh blanket at her feet, sieved flour has piled up in a small cone.

Several small insects have wriggled clear of the cone, having miraculously survived the quern and the millstones. The corpses of other less fortunate insects can be seen mixed into the flour on the rug. In the weak light of the early dawn the grandmother cannot see the insects until Lan scoops up a handful of flour and holds it in front of the old woman's face.

Even when she can finally see the insects, the grandmother does not see that to be a problem. She shrugs, observing that the bugs must have got into the storage vats when they were left open after the recent rain. Lan has to admit that when she was digging the grain out of the bottom of the vat, it did feel rather damp.

'Well,' remarks the old lady, 'we can't use that flour for our ancestors now. Still, the flour is perfectly good for our daily food. The insects are harmless, so there's really no reason to do anything.'

Over her mother-in-law's shoulder, Lan sees her daughter's jaw drop in shock. She ignores Mei's silent – but very urgent – gestures, and brings the conversation back to what they should now offer their ancestors on the morrow. Perhaps the insects in the flour are a sign that the idea of using last year's grain was misguided. Thereafter, the three agree that they will take the damp new grain, bake it at the hearth until it is dry, and then grind it into flour. This involves more work for everyone, but it seems there is not much else they can do.

Lan walks back to the house, leaving her daughter and mother-in-law to discuss re-arranging their domestic tasks to make time for this extra chore. Everyone else in the household will be waking up soon, and she has to prepare breakfast and then work out how to persuade her daughter to eat anything for the next month.

The Bronze
Worker Consults
a Colleague

When Huang has set up his workshop for the
morning's tasks, he goes over to see his friend
Long. Yet when he arrives, his friend is so
assiduously polishing his bronze ruler that he does not notice
Huang's arrival. Not that it would make any difference
anyway – Long owes his reputation for precise, meticulous
work in part to the precise measurements densely marked
in different scales on both the long and short sides of his
L-shaped ruler. He would not stop polishing even if he had
noted Huang's arrival.

Stepping closer, Huang reads the inscription painted on
the long side of the ruler: '*jiu shi*' (meaning 'ninety'). Some
workmen need to replace their tools every few months, but
that ruler has been with Long for over a decade now. The
instrument is well-worn but it shines as though brand new
– partly, Huang knows, because the alloy used for the ruler
was low in tin, so the ruler is almost pure copper. This means

that it bends easily, and whenever that happens Long curses energetically and has to set aside time to beat it straight and flat once more. Even more annoying is that, over time, the measurement scales carefully calibrated onto the side of the ruler wear away, meaning that Long has to use an iron knife to re-carve the tiny markings, and then smooth down the ruler's surface with cloth and animal fat.

Huang has a wooden ruler, which does the job of measuring with reasonable precision, doesn't bend, and is easily replaced if it should snap. But he always calibrates his rulers against Long's, replicating the tiny 'x' every five notches that indicates a measurement equal to an inch, a pattern repeated right along the ruler's edge. However, there is no way that Huang is also going to replicate the beautiful geometric patterns on the other side of the ruler – his wooden rulers don't last long enough to make the effort worthwhile. Soon perhaps, Huang will get a bone ruler; he recently saw one decorated with lively carved images, and now he is on the lookout for something similar.

INK RUBBING OF A STONE-RELIEF CARVING SHOWING WHAT IS LIKELY TO BE THE LEGENDARY FIGURES OF FUXI AND NÜWA HOLDING RULERS AND MEASURING, AD 151

Both Long and Huang are bronze-mirror makers, and often a top-quality ruler, tastefully decorated, is used where a cheap wooden ruler would suffice for making the design on the back of the mirrors. It's a prestige thing that helps a worker stand out in the state-run factory where the two have spent their entire working lives.

That lifetime in state employment would probably not be the case were Huang and his friend twenty years younger. When the two started their careers, bronze was produced under a strict government monopoly, so a bronze worker had no choice but to work for the state. But there have been changes recently and government control is loosening, not only over the bronze industry but also with the former state monopolies controlling the production of salt and iron. Rich merchants and feudal lords have sensed that there are profits to be made, starting with expensive and prestigious items – such as bronze mirrors produced by the likes of Huang and Long.

Suddenly bronze-working has become a vibrant industry, powered by a new flexibility combined with technological advances. Unlike the bronze-making industry before Han, which mainly fashioned ritual vessels under the auspices of the state, private workshops were now leading the way forward, while wealthy opportunists 'sponsored' state workshops, as this allowed them to take orders and customize products for their customers. Naturally, these new private workshops were keen to poach skilled workers from the government industry, and other bronze-mirror makers had set themselves up in business on their own account. Many of these entrepreneurs had done well enough to now be seriously wealthy, and hardly a month went by without both Huang and Long receiving lucrative offers from the private sector.

So far, Huang has persuaded Long to stay with the state factory, pointing out that over the decades he has seen ebbs and flows in the demand for bronze work, especially mirrors. It would be foolish to abandon their safe jobs just as the market for mirrors peaked and the inevitable crash and unemployment followed. Anyway, as Huang likes to remark, wealth just means you have more money – in their stratified world, a wealthy craftsman is still just a craftsman, excluded from the society and privileges of his 'betters'.

After work, Long and Huang sometimes sit over a beaker or two of rice wine and discuss the role and status of craftsmen in the state. It is difficult to grasp the state's attitude towards skilled artisans such as themselves – men incapable of crafting a line of decent poetry to save their lives, but of far more value to the economy than many of those who could.

Huang is very suspicious about all these new changes. 'Not good, not good,' he always says, shaking his head like a senile old man. Long is more positive, pointing out that there is more working space in the shop after some workers have left, and in an attempt to keep those workers who remain, management has greatly improved their working conditions. It is a good time to be a craftsman.

This morning Huang has come to Long for a consultation, for he needs to make a mirror tomorrow and his manager has given very specific instructions about how it is to be done. Huang is not happy about taking instruction from a man who has never crafted a mirror in his life, especially since those instructions seem to make little sense. In order for the proposed mirror to be as close as possible to the silver-whitish colour considered ideal, the manager has asked Huang to make the alloy half copper and half tin – which to Huang seems less a recipe for an alloy than for disaster.

Royal craftsmen

Written during the Warring States period (*c.* fifth century BC) by someone in the Qi state, *Kao Gong Ji* (*Records of Examination of Craftsmen*) is the earliest detailed account of royal craftsmanship in ancient China. Its encyclopaedic records document different ways of life for royalty, officers, craftsmen, merchants, farmers and female workers. The section on craftsmen includes seven tasks for woodworkers (e.g., pole making), six jobs for metal workers (e.g., bell founding), five for leatherworkers (e.g., skinning and drum making), and other tasks for embroiderers, jade-workers, potters and others. Profoundly influential among royal artisans in the Han period, the *Kao Gong Ji* contains six recipes for alloys (*liu ji*) for casting in different kinds of bronze products. From scientific analysis of archaeologically recovered metal objects it is clear that the content of the alloys broadly agrees with the formulas described in the text.

Long confirms Huang's forebodings. 'Don't listen to him! I have tried making the alloy half tin. You get a bright colour that an optimist might consider white, but you won't have long to admire it – those mirrors are extremely delicate and one good bump turns them into a pile of shards on the floor.'

While he is talking, Long stands and takes down one of the long wooden boxes he calls his 'treasure chests'. Long has two of these because he is an inveterate experimenter, and he likes to keep samples from each experiment as a reminder of what went right and what went wrong. It is a sort of reference guide for his work; one of the reasons that Huang enjoys sitting beside his friend and talking about bronze casting is that

Long is always able to fish out a relevant alloy to demonstrate his point.

Now Long digs up a piece of broken mirror from a pile of slag and scrap products and shows it to Huang. 'The manager probably does not even know that when casting the decorative motifs on the back you also need to add a small amount of lead to increase the fluidity of the alloy. So just to comply with his instructions you need to make the alloy half tin and also not half tin. I suppose he did not instruct you on how to achieve this impossible feat?' asks Long rhetorically.

The new mirror has not yet even been started, and already Huang feels a strong dislike for the product. He clutches a sketch of leather in one hand, and now he shows this to Long. It is a dragon pattern that the manager has insisted that Huang cast on the back of the mirror, with the dragon depicted in a multitude of fine lines that promise hours of trouble for the person doing the casting.

To cast a bronze mirror one needs two moulds – one for the face of the mirror and another for the back, and it is the back cast that is the more troublesome. A good alloy usually can be made into a good mirror, but fine lines on the back mould do not always come out well in the final cast, emerging instead as a blurry mockery of the original concept. Casting such lines properly requires getting the gap between the two moulds exactly right, for if the gap is too narrow or uneven the molten alloy will not flow smoothly through the lines in the mould nor cool off evenly afterwards. And such is the uncertainty in the bronze crafter's art that one can do everything exactly right and still end up with an inexplicably flawed cast.

It is not that Huang, with his years of experience, doubts he will be able to manage to cast the fine lines, but the task will be tedious and time-consuming. Furthermore, the finished dragon would be the height of fashion – twenty years ago. Today's fashion is for the symmetric designs of *Boju* mirrors, geometric patterns that, in Huang's opinion, are both inspiring and aesthetically superior (and much easier to cast.)

These *Boju* mirrors remind Huang of the Mingtang and Piyong ceremonial buildings outside Chang'an city. They have the same design as the pattern on the back of these mirrors – a circular periphery with a square shape contained within. Apparently, even the central building in the complex has the same design, though, as a lowly craftsman, Huang has never been permitted to go inside. The 'square within a circle' is becoming a popular motif – even some coins now carry it.

While Huang is considering these matters, Long reaches into his treasure chest once more and pulls out a clay mould for the back of a mirror he made a few days ago. Naturally, the

A BRONZE *BOJU* MIRROR

mould is broken, because clay moulds are used only once. The average craftsman simply smashes his mould when he is done with it. Huang muses that only a perfectionist would break the mould exactly down the middle and then preserve the two halves for future reference.

Huang takes the mould and puts the two broken pieces together, seeing how the lines stand out clearly in the yellowish clay, even though stained by the slightly oxidized slag of the mirror. A deep hole in the middle of the mould is surrounded by a square-shaped groove. The perfectly shaped hole and groove are used to cast the characteristic round knob of the *Boju* mirror and its accompanying square ridge.

Most clay moulds are of standard material – a porous, sandy clay paste – but Huang notices that Long's mould contains evenly distributed voids formed by burned rice chaff that the craftsman has added to make the mould light and easily permeated by air during the casting process.

It is because they take such care with the preparation of their moulds that Huang and Long are given much of the factory's custom work. Those workers who mass-produce mirrors need no such skills because the manager will simply give them a parent mould for the type of mirror he wants to have churned out. All that such workers need to do is to prepare their clay and make a mould of the parent mould, then use that to cast the actual mirror. Being undamaged, the parent mould can be used again and again, and afterwards all the workman needs to do is carefully finish the motifs once the mirror has been cast.

The mould that Huang holds is of a different level altogether, and it is only by peering closely that Huang can count the small circles inside and outside each square that were used to create the small bronze nubs that give the back of the mirror its distinctive character.

Boju mirrors

The *Boju* mirror is sometimes called the TLV mirror, because the motif patterns in different parts of the mirror resemble the letters T, L and V in Roman script. While bronze mirrors with a similar design have been found in a tomb of 104 BC, it was not until Wang Mang's era that this style became popular. There is a growing consensus that this popular design was used by Wang Mang, the 'usurper' emperor, to spread his political propaganda. Some Wang-Mang-era *Boju* mirrors have inscriptions on them praising the emperor's achievements, such as the building of the Mingtang and Piyong ceremonial temples, and his forcing the troublesome Xiongnu Huns to submit to the Han.

From his other treasure chest, Long takes out a bronze mirror, which he proudly presents to Huang. He confesses that he was not going to show it just yet, as he needs to polish and refine the back a bit more, but the finished model is easier for Huang to appreciate than having to extrapolate the shape of the mirror-back from its mould.

A dozen small nubs lie parallel to the four sides of the internal square of the *Boju* mirror-back. Outside the square, another eight nubs form a circle surrounding the square, for as Long often says, a good *Boju* mirror-back is all about playing with the variations and contrasts of circle and square.

The mirror is a marvel of intricate design and fine craftsmanship, which Long has given an extra dimension to by adding a circle of small triangular ridges to the edge of the mirror. As a fellow craftsman, Huang can appreciate the precision with which the small triangles are perfectly aligned with one another, with the inward-facing triangles pointing to another circle of swirling patterns. It is because he likes to produce work of this standard that Long is obsessed with his bronze ruler.

Long's mastery of geometry reminds Huang of another problem that he wants to talk over with his colleague. As the craftsman who produces better geometric patterns than anyone else in the factory, Long might know the answer to a problem that Huang has encountered with another of his moulds – he needs to divide a circle into seven equal parts, and he cannot figure out how to do this.

One can bisect a circle with a straight line across the middle, and a trisection is easily accomplished with a compass. And once you have halves or thirds, sixths, eighths and other equal divisions of a circle are easily drawn. Long uses his own mirror-back as an example – just draw straight lines between any two random nubs inside the square and two outside plus the knob in the middle, and this divides the circle into as many even-numbered sections as the designer might wish. Huang knows this, but waits patiently, for he knows from experience that it is easier to let Long approach an explanation in his own way.

Finally, Long gets to the point, saying, 'There is no easy way to draw dividing lines for seven equal parts. I would normally adjust the diameters of the compass and repeatedly join the points until I find the seven equal dividing points on the circle.'

This explanation leaves Huang more than somewhat confused, for Long is better at doing these things than he is at explaining them. Huang decides that he needs to have Long come over to his work bench and demonstrate the process upon his mould. This will have to wait until tomorrow, for now that he has prepared his ruler, Long is about to embark on making a mould of his own. This is a standard job, and one that will not take him long.

Huang is unable to work on his circle mould until Long has shown him the technique, and the mirror with the dragon-back is going to have to wait until Huang has patiently explained to the manager why the alloy mix he wants is not going to work. This means that Huang has the leisure to sit back and watch his colleague in action.

Long walks to the well outside his shed and fills a water bottle, which he then empties into a shallow pit that contains clay and fine white sand. The clay and sand in the pit have already been thoroughly mixed, and Long just wants to moisturize it.

Once the mixture has been kneaded into a paste, Long puts it on his working platform and fishes out a parent mould from his treasure case. Although this parent mould has clearly been used and re-used many times, it remains in good condition thanks to Long's meticulous maintenance. Most parent moulds develop holes, scratches and other imperfections on the surface, but this mould remains smooth. The raised parts on the two ends of the mould – where the feeder and pouring heads are fitted – seem particularly well looked after, with not even a tiny trace of clay stuck to them.

Long quickly spreads the clay paste onto the parent mould, massaging it into an upside-down bowl shape just over an inch thick. While the clay dries, Huang assumes that Long will prepare the furnace in which he will bake the mould, but instead Long starts spreading a thin layer of black material onto where the mirror face will be.

'What is that?' Huang asks curiously.

'I think there are two main requirements for the successful casting of a product,' his colleague replies. 'One is that the clay mould is baked at the right temperature; the other that, after it has been made, the mould must be properly preheated before the molten alloy is poured in. This ensures that the alloy cools down smoothly – otherwise you get bubbles, and bubbles produce defects.

'A few days ago,' he continues, 'I heard that if you spread a thin layer of heat-resistant material onto the clay mould, this will help to ensure that the mould will break apart safely without cracking the mirror. I damaged a bronze mirror the other day when the mirror and clay mould were stuck to each other too tightly. So now I'm going to try this technique on a mirror I can re-cast quickly if something goes wrong. If it works, I'll use it on some of my more expensive customized mirrors.'

Huang ponders this. It would not be a bad idea, he feels, to apply this method to the dragon-motif mirror the manager wants, so he decides to head back to his workbench and start work on the dragon sketches in the hope of getting them outlined before lunch.

'Come back tomorrow and check my results,' Long calls after Huang's retreating back.

The Canal Worker is Nostalgic

The barge moves slowly forward against the current as Tian poles it upstream. On either side of the barge, workers plunge their long-handled spades into the canal bottom. As they work loose the heavy clay, they chant '*yi-ya*', sounding to Tian rather like a collection of barnyard cockerels. The penetrating grunts and groans of the workers echo through the mist, broken only by the rhythmic smack of the dug-out lumps of wet clay as they land in the bamboo baskets on the barge.

It's only May and already Tian and his fellow workers are working to clear the bed of the canal. Winter storms – and summer thunderstorms – flush rubbish and sediment into the rivers, and this all tends to settle in the more placid waters of Tian's stretch of canal. No one objected when their supervisor decided that they should make an early start on canal clearance this year, because the crew have learned over time that keeping the canal clear is in their own best interest. The more smoothly that traffic moves through their stretch of the canal, the less likely it is that boats will get stranded and others backed up behind the stranded vessel. In turn, this means fewer emergencies or general chaos for Tian and his crew to sort out.

Canals are the key to the transport system of the entire empire. Every day and night thousands of barges and ships are on the move through the empire's network of rivers and canals, carrying people, food, construction material and trade goods. Tian is proud of the work that he does. He might be merely the tiniest of cogs in a vast machine, but that machine keeps the empire operating. At any given moment, hundreds of thousands of labourers like himself are at work on the canals of the empire, clearing obstacles, rescuing stranded ships, and on occasion pulling cargo from a boat that has actually capsized, then securing the flotsam on the banks.

Just as there are different types of canal, so there are different types of canal workers. Tian is forever grateful that he avoided being conscripted to work on the notorious Dizhu canal, unaffectionately known to those who serve there as the 'Gateway to Hell'. Located near the Sanmen Gorge, this notorious canal is the busiest and most lethal stretch of water in the empire's enormous transportation system. The Yellow River takes a sharp bend here, smashing its waters hard against a reef that breaks up the river as the waters rage past. This creates chaotic white water and dangerous, unseen undercurrents that regularly claim boats and the lives of their crews. 'Hit the reef, smashed into powder, vanished in the swirl'; this laconic epitaph is one that canal workers have given to so many lost ships that it has become almost a catchphrase among them.

Operating this stretch of waterway is none too safe for the workers either, as Tian can attest. One of his relatives successfully avoided being sent there year after year, but eventually that canal's need for manpower caused the courts to order the relative's conscription. The poor man lasted a matter of months before slipping on a treacherous stone path on the cliffs above the canal. Once he fell into the water he was doomed. Swept away, he is presumed drowned, for his body was never found.

Canal work is dangerous, and hard. Thousands of workers, many of them criminals or conscripts, died building this section of the Dizhu canal, chiselling out narrow paths across the sheer rock faces and dangling by precarious makeshift bridges above the turbulent waters. Yet the Dizhu is only an extreme example of the dangers that all canal workers face.

Tian lives at a work camp situated further west, on an alluvial bar overlooking the floodplain alongside the southern bank of the Wei River. Whereas the Yellow River is dangerous because of its roaring waters, the Wei is downright lazy. A straight road between the Wei and Yellow Rivers would only be a hundred *li* or so, but the Wei River meanders through almost ten times that distance. The slow waters easily become clogged with sediment, and the lazy coils of the waterway create unpredictable currents and shifting mud banks that are a constant menace to shipping.

Yet the Wei River is an essential link between the flourishing eastern parts of the empire and the capital at Chang'an. Every day, hundreds of boats make their way to the city, bringing food and the myriad other goods the city needs to function. Eventually, the exasperated authorities became tired of heavily loaded ships continually getting bogged down on the river's mud-flats and petitioned the Emperor Wu (157–87 BC) for permission to straighten the river with a canal.

Tian proudly tells strangers that 'his' canal was created in three short years by tens of thousands of labourers brought in for the project. The job significantly shortened the journey of 900 *li* (450 km) along the unreliable waters of the Wei to a 300-*li* trip down the Caoqu canal. As a bonus, the project has already extended irrigation to hundreds of thousands of acres of arable land alongside it. Workers such as Tian have the task of making sure that the passage of the barges is easy and uninterrupted. His crew are responsible for 11 *li* of the canal.

Tian was one of the workers who moved north to work on the project. He was originally at a ship-building factory on the banks of the Yellow River at Mengjin. However, this new post is closer to his home, and when he was recruited by the Ministry his new job came with the administrative title of *chuansigong*. Impressive as this title may be, it does not excuse Tian from the heavy labour expected of a canal worker. His routine duties include dredging and cleaning the canal bottom, and even on occasion unloading the barges at the docks.

Also, of course, it is not uncommon for Tian and his workers to be roused from their beds in the middle of the night because some incompetent pilot has steered his barge into the canal bank or run it aground on a mudflat. On such occasions, the crew take out their own barge and try to tow the boats out of trouble, or they climb into the water and try to shove a trapped barge off the glue-like clay and back into the main current of the 80-m-wide canal.

Because of his experience with boat-building, Tian was awarded the job of steersman for the barge. Now, everyone automatically assumes that, as they approach their boat, Tian will be the one to take up the long bamboo pole that is used for both propulsion and steering. Tian also keeps a shorter paddle under his bench for those occasions when extra power is needed. Rowing and poling his barge along the canal have given Tian arms so corded with muscle that these days he thinks nothing of dragging the barge from the canal to the bank

THIS POTTERY MODEL IS AN EARLY EXAMPLE OF A BOAT WITH A RUDDER, AN IMPORTANT INVENTION OF THE EASTERN HAN DYNASTY

without assistance. He rather likes his job, though he also thinks it would be nice if some extra pay accompanied the extra responsibility he has taken on.

Today, they started work early in the morning, the fog swirling about them as they gathered at a claw-like barrage on the canal bank. These barrages are made from long-bladed grasses and small twigs with an overlay of dark earth. They are used to raise water levels and divert the flow of the canal. One feature of their canal is a parallel channel that turns north-west back to the Wei River, reducing the time that barges must spend going upstream. It's an ingenious system, and Tian often thinks that the designers and engineers responsible for this marvel of hydraulic engineering deserve far more recognition. Here, after all, is a giant river that has been tamed for the benefit of the empire's people – not only does it now supply irrigation and transport, but the addition of the canal has mitigated the disastrous floods that ruined the crops of so many farmers in previous generations.

At present, most of the barrages are matted tightly to the canal bank, and one of these is currently serving the canal crew as a makeshift jetty. Their barge was moored on the downstream side of the barrage, and so dense had been the clammy morning mist that Tian had almost stepped off the edge of the platform when he came to untie the hemp mooring rope from its large wooden stake. Although the barrage has made the currents near the mooring more predictable, there have been a few occasions when the boat was washed away immediately by swiftly changing currents after it was released from the stake.

Tian keeps a wary eye on the workers – they are quickly filling the bamboo baskets with clay, painfully laborious as the task seems to be. He knows from experience that should they become too preoccupied with what they are doing and congregate on one side of the boat, the barge will capsize. Tian knows that he's not at fault on such occasions, but he certainly doesn't like it happening and is not above using his steering pole to nudge his team back to their proper positions.

The upstream part of the job is done and Tian poles the barge back downstream to where the waters of the canal are shallower. They reach the barrage, and the workers jump off

Hydraulic innovations

Li Bing (*c.* third century BC) is perhaps China's greatest hydraulic engineer. It was he who cleverly designed the renowned Dujiangyan hydraulic system on the Min River, which successfully prevented floods and irrigated paddy fields in the Chengdu plain for several hundred years, and which continued to function through the following millennia.

to collect the clay baskets that Tian hands to them. Clay is a nuisance on the canal bottom, but elsewhere it's a valuable resource, and other workers will soon come along to collect the baskets. What they do with them Tian neither knows nor cares. The clay is no longer interfering with traffic along his stretch of canal, and that's all he is concerned about.

As the barge is slowly poled upstream once more, the sun starts to break through. From his position on the raised stern of the barge Tian sees the large form of a passing ship taking shape in the dispersing mist. With an expert glance he quickly assesses the ship's tonnage and length. As an experienced shipbuilder he reckons this is one of the five *zhang* ships. They are approximately 11.5 m long and of variable width, the wider ones able to carry 500 *dan* (stone) of grain or other goods.

There's a chant from the rowers powering the ship down the canal, and from the sound of it there are a good number of them. As the ship approaches, Tian sees that it has eight sets of oars, fixed to tholepins within the hull. In unison, the oars slice through the water like swords. As the boat goes rapidly by, Tian notes that on its stern is a rudder-like device that controls the ship's direction. He gazes at it, intrigued. He has heard of these things, but has never seen one in operation. It's impossible not to be impressed by how steadily the ship holds its course, even though it is being rowed at a good speed.

'That ship must have come from the dockyards in the south,' he tells the other workers as he points out the rudder. 'They're smart down there. They build really good, fast vessels.'

'Are you getting nostalgic for your former job as a shipbuilder?' one of the workers asks teasingly, but before Tian can answer, the bow waves from the ship reach them, fast and heavy enough to rock the barge violently and push it to the side of the canal. Tian and the workers jump onto the bank to lighten the load, and watch the large ship recede into the mist.

As they watch, Tian tells the others of the different types of vessels he once worked on in Mengjin. The most luxurious was a five-deck cabin, another was a battleship made with a wire framework, another was actually two ships lashed together side by side. His reminiscences become increasingly animated until he notes the concerned glances being exchanged by the others. He quickly reassures them, 'Sure I miss the old days at the shipyard, but I am also pleased with what I am doing now. This work is important, isn't it?'

Reminded of the task at hand, they refresh themselves from their water flasks and resume work, keeping close to the banks of the canal. The '*yin-ya*' work chant breaks out again as spadefuls of sticky clay are hauled from the bed of the canal. The chant is suddenly interrupted by the sound of wood splintering as a wooden haft breaks, leaving the head of the spade embedded in the mud of the canal bottom. Work stops as the crew survey the damage.

Tian glares at his fellow workers, but none of them seem inclined to move. True, the ministry would eventually replace the spade head, but it is iron, and iron parts are slow to arrive – if they ever do. These spades are specialized instruments specifically designed for shifting riverine clay. Each spade has two tines, which break up the clay on the river bottom. The workers keep these tines sharp, which makes retrieving the spade head a dangerous task as well as an unpleasant one.

It is not Tian's job to fish out the broken implement, but every second they spend debating the matter takes them further downstream and makes the spade harder to locate in the muddy water, so in the end Tian decides to get the spade head himself and give his fellow workers a lecture later.

Though the water is not deep, it is remarkably chilly. Also, Tian has forgotten to roll up his trouser legs, and now they will be covered with clay from the canal bottom. In fact Tian's first job is to free his feet from the same clinging clay. He shuffles forward, feeling the sticky stuff squelching through his toes as he searches using both feet and hands. He is now wet through and largely covered in mud. Fortunately, his questing toes feel the metal edge of the spade before he has searched for long.

Without speaking, Tian throws the spade onto the barge and pushes it to the bank. While one worker heads back to the camp to get a new spade, Tian and the others unload the half-laden barge and take a moment to catch their breath. Then Tian goes to the canal edge to wash. As he does so, another ship glides down towards them, and Tian cranes his neck to see it better. The other workers wait for Tian's commentary on what they are seeing. But this time he is silent, watching with a wistful, faraway look in his dark eyes.

辰 SECOND HOUR OF THE DAY

(07.00–08.00: THE FIRST PART OF *CHEN*)

THE TEACHER STARTS HIS CLASS

The master said, 'The silent treasuring up of knowledge; learning without satiety; and instructing others without being wearied: which one of these things belongs to me?'

Shu'er chapter, *Analects of Confucius*

The most prestigious position in the classroom faces east towards the morning sun, and because the sun has been up for over an hour, sunlight floods the classroom. Naturally, the prestigious east-facing position is occupied by the teacher, who has a raised platform as a further demonstration of his authority. Here Wen sits and sourly regards his fifteen students, who look back with bleary eyes and weary expressions that accurately indicate the class had too little sleep and too much wine last night.

This is not the first time this has happened, nor even the first time this month. Wen is in charge of the county school of the Runan prefecture. As an alternative to the *Taixue* Imperial Academy in the central court, schools such as his receive financial support and sponsorships from various levels, from the emperor to local governors. Consequently, most of Wen's students are either from wealthy families or are otherwise connected to the aristocratic and political elite of the prefecture.

Yesterday, there was another social gathering attended by his students and the local gentry, and as part of the festivities the *Boshi* students had rehearsed for the upcoming *sheli* archery ritual. Wen well knows that at these events large quantities of wine are supplied, which his young charges happily consume. He is not against such social gatherings and he agrees that these soirées play a key role in keeping up student morale and getting the youths used to appropriate behaviour in a social setting. Indeed, if he had been invited, Wen would willingly have helped to set up the target and assisted the students in practising their archery. But he was not invited, possibly because he feels strongly that partying at such events ought to have limits, particularly for the young, and especially for his students.

Wen instead passed a restrained and decent evening yesterday alone at home with his wife, and perhaps for this reason his pupils' sagging faces particularly irritate him this morning. Look at them all, like wilted wildflowers – they can't even sit upright, their eyes are dull, and their hats are crooked, jammed onto their heads any old how!

Wen's many frustrations start bubbling to the surface, and leaping to his feet he runs to a partition at the side of the classroom where an image of Confucius is painted. A suppressed snigger from a student reminds him that running is against the very code of etiquette he has been trying to drum into the class, so he pauses abruptly and walks with forced elegance the rest of the way to the partition.

The front of the partition portrays the famous scene where Confucius met Laozi in his journey to the Zhou court to study

Zhou rites. The painting on the back is a vivid depiction of Confucius asking a question of a child. The paintings on both sides successfully capture the bookish Confucius's humble attitude towards learning.

Wen points at the portraits forcefully while he harangues his pupils. 'Look at the sage: his clothing is proper, his hat is tidy, and his gestures suitably display his righteousness!' Angrily, the teacher repeats the words of the Master: 'In a hamlet of ten households, there are bound to be those who are my equal in doing their best for others and being trustworthy in what they say, but they are unlikely to be as eager to learn as I am.' Can't Wen's students see that learning is a privilege that even the great Confucius sought eagerly?

He whirls back to face his class, knowing full well that while he'd been speaking some pupils were grimacing behind his back, while others were mouthing his words with exaggerated gestures. The class look back with feigned innocence as Wen stands fuming in silent frustration. Oh, how he would love to give each and every one of them a thrashing – a proper beating, comprehensive enough to focus the minds of the poorly behaved, disrespectful rabble he is attempting to educate. He would be within his rights to do so, but his wife has always stopped him, cautioning that some of these young men will hold positions of high authority in the future. The beaten student of today may well be tomorrow's bureaucrat with a grudge, so Wen has to restrain his authoritarian instincts.

It is inevitable that some of the class, for all their oafish behaviour and manners, will become the future *Boshi* students in the imperial court. Consequently, Wen knows that he would be well advised to heed his wife's warnings. He himself has noticed that the government has a tendency to prefer officials with formal educational backgrounds from schools such as his – indeed, this is the main reason that such schools have been prospering across the counties and prefectures of the empire. Over the years, an increasing number of Confucian students from his region have gone into the court and taken important jobs.

Boshi students

Boshi was originally used to refer to knowledgeable intellectuals or scholars. It became an official title during the Qin era. During Emperor Wu's reign, the *wujing* (Five Classic canons) *Boshi* title was established to promote the education of Confucian canons. The Five Classics included *Shijing* (*Classic of Poetry*), *Shangshu* (*Book of Documents*), *Li* (*Rites of Zhou*), *Yi* (*Book of Changes*), and *Chunqiu* (*Spring and Autumn Annals*).

Numerous *wujing Boshi* scholars who were proficient in these canons sprang up after the promotion of Emperor Wu and his most important officer, Dong Zhongshu. Emperor Wu's establishment of the *wujing Boshi* system also brought some reform of the selection process, which was thereafter limited exclusively to Confucian students and scholars.

Because the bureaucracy increasingly draws recruits from Confucian students, the new emperor Wang Mang has refined and improved the student selection process. (A positive step, Wen feels, though his own class demonstrates that the process can still be improved much further.) The emperor has also expanded the study list of Confucian canons and set up new positions for the *Boshi* students.

As a result, Wen and his peers are aware that the relationship between teachers and students is changing. Indeed, Wen himself needs to adapt to the shifting governmental policies on education. As Confucius himself said, 'The mechanic, who wishes to do his work well, must first sharpen his tools.' As soon as he gets some free time, Wen plans to learn some other Confucian classics apart from the standard *Shijing* and *Shangshu* texts. He firmly believes that a person's conscientiousness and integrity can be deeply shaped by a comprehensive education in the Confucian canon.

Theoretically, thanks to the new imperial policy, Wen can now educate many more successful students, who will in due course enter into the court and eventually become a positive influence on the imperial bureaucracy. In practice it is not an easy task educating fifteen teenage boys, and usually Wen gets a major headache in exchange for every minor bit of Confucian wisdom that he imparts to his troublesome brats.

A few of the more senior boys are becoming particularly difficult to discipline. When Wen's back is turned, they throw things at each other, climb on top of each other playing dangerous games, mess up each other's clothing with black ink, or break the ink slab or other objects used for writing. Generally, Wen hides his silent fury behind an impassive mask, though everyone recalls his epic explosion when his students went too far and tried to paint over the image of the Duke of Zhou and Confucius on the wall.

The intellectual performance of the fifteen pupils in the school varies widely. One young pupil, Meng, has been particularly excellent in his studies. Whenever Wen asks questions from the classic texts, Meng is always the first to put up his hand and answer. His recitations of the *Zuo Zhuan* (*The Commentary of Zuo*) are impressively articulate. Wen has high hopes for this boy and his future. This morning he plans to ask the student to recite and interpret the *Lun Yun* (*The Analects of Confucius*).

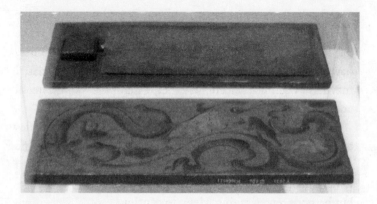

Inkstone in a lacquer case

For this reason he has decided to play the *shece* game at the start of today's lessons, rather than waiting until the end of the day as he normally does. Last night – while his class were out partying – he had carefully written ten questions on wooden plaques and covered them with plates by the small platform where he sits.

He announces to the class, 'You have been studying and revising the *Lun Yu* for quite a long time now. Today we are going to see how well you can remember the analects between the sage and his students and how insightful your interpretation is.'

He thought the pupils would cheer at this announcement, as they would normally do whenever they were told they were going to play a game, but to his disappointment nobody responds with any enthusiasm. Wen looks over at Meng, who can usually be counted on to greet his suggestions warmly, but this time Meng ducks his head and looks away.

Nevertheless, if anyone is going to get the *shece* game properly started it is Meng, so Wen calls the student and tells him to draw a plaque from the platform and, once it is uncovered, read the quotation from the *Lun Yu* out loud.

'The *Xue'er Learning* chapter. "Zeng Zi said, I daily examine myself on three points." Interpret.' Meng recites the rest of the quotation. '… whether, in transacting business for others, I may have been not faithful; whether, in intercourse with friends, I may have been not sincere; whether, I may have not mastered and practised the instructions of my teacher?'

For his interpretation, the studious young pupil decides to articulate the bold approach he has been pondering. 'The master here refers to learning, friendship and gentlemen.' Wen looks somewhat startled at the interposition of the 'gentlemen' but he nods, encouraging Meng to continue.

'A gentleman aspires to learn. That's how a gentleman acquires *dao* and *ren* benevolence through learning. As I read the *Yang Huo* chapter, the master has said that when the man of high station is well instructed, he loves men; when the man of low station is well instructed, he is easily ruled.' Wen is pleased with Meng's answer and deems the commentary sound, concise and eloquent.

He is especially impressed by Meng's quotation of a *Yang Huo* chapter, which he has not yet taught to the class. Still, Wen probes deeper, both to check the depth of Meng's understanding and for the elucidation of his fellow students. 'What about friendship and being a gentleman; why is that important?'

Meng considers for a while and replies, 'The Zeng Zi said, "The gentleman on grounds of culture meets with his friends, and by their friendship helps his … virtue".'

As Meng is returning to his seat Wen addresses the class as a whole. 'The master said that there are three things of which the gentleman stands in awe. He stands in awe of the ordinances of Heaven. He stands in awe of great men. He stands in awe of the words of sages. The master adds that he also is fearful of three losses …'

Wen's commentary is abruptly interrupted by a sharp clang from one side of the room. The source of the sound is a bronze bottle and its lid rolling along the floor towards a corner. A pupil is kneeling on the floor scrambling after the runaway objects. In stony silence Wen watches as the boy retrieves the bottle, replaces the lid, and puts it back on the shelf. The teacher does not ask what has happened because this is not the first time that the student in question has been caught fiddling with objects in the classroom when he should have been listening to Wen speak.

So now Wen turns to his errant pupil and tells him to step forward and draw out a plaque. 'The Zeng Zi said, "Let there be … hmm, a careful attention to perform the funeral rites to … parents … and let them be followed … umm, when long gone … with the ceremonies of sacrifice, then the virtue of the people will … er … resume its proper excellence."'

The reading is accurate, if not exactly fluent, so Wen waits to see how the student will interpret the quotation, but the lad had evidently exhausted his intellectual capacity and he now just stands there like a pole, scratching his head and saying nothing.

'The sage fears three losses.' Wen takes the opportunity to pick up his commentary from before he was rudely interrupted. 'One of these losses came when he toured around all the kingdoms and returned to find that he had lost his parents. The tree wishes to be still, yet the wind continues to blow; the son wants to fulfil his duty to his mother and father, but they are with him no longer.'

Wen is pleased that he has had the opportunity to insert this point into the lesson. The government is keen on teachers promoting the idea of filial piety, and Wen and his fellow teachers are agreed that if the *Boshi* students are to become more respectful to their parents, they should do so with reference to the classic canons on the subject.

To hammer this point into the minds of the class (Wen has long ago given up the idea that subtlety might work) he instructs them to write the sentence down on their bamboo scrolls and memorize it.

The room is studiously quiet for all of several seconds before there comes the sudden sound of a brittle object breaking. In the middle row of the class a student has somehow managed to snap the leg off his ink tray and the spilled ink is turning his sleeves black. The student seated next to him pretends to help as he deliberately makes the situation worse by spilling the ink over the matting on the floor.

Wen looks at the mess, noting that the now ruined ink tray had been decorated with a beautifully carved animal shape. It's no loss to him personally, for the students bring their own writing material to the school (and that material brought by students from wealthy families is often ostentatiously valuable). The ink tray was one that Wen would have been proud to own, and it makes his heart ache to see it so carelessly vandalized. Forcing himself to patience, he instructs the two students to share an ink tray so that they will not lag behind the rest of the class.

When the emperor Wang Mang was a young visiting student to the famous Confucian scholar Chen Can, Wang wore full Confucian dress and behaved in a proper Confucian manner. Wen thinks that Wang Mang's success is due to his attention to detail, and he is convinced that if his students had to wear proper Confucian robes they might finally start acting like proper Confucian students. Instead … well … Wen sighs, noting that the lesson has just started and he has many hours yet to get through before he has seen the last of his students for the day.

THE TEXTILE
WORKER PICKS
MULBERRY LEAVES

After working through yet another late night, Le had planned to stay in bed a bit longer this morning. So she groans softly to herself as her mother storms in just as the dawn is breaking. 'Lazy girl, wake up! The basket of mulberry leaves is almost empty. Can't you see that there are only a few leaves left?'

Le forces herself awake and rather groggily goes to inspect the basket sitting outside on the windowsill. Sure enough, there are only a few leaves scattered on the bottom of the basket, and even these look dry and shrivelled. The family's silkworms won't much like those leaves for their breakfast, and it is one of Le's household chores to keep the basket topped up. Without comment, the girl collects the basket and goes out into the chilly freshness of the morning.

Her mother was right to remind her to refill the basket, Le thinks, but she hates the way her mother still treats her as a child even though she has been doing an adult's work for these past few months.

Le smiles to herself as she thinks of yesterday's tiring but pleasant evening. Much of her enjoyment came not just from the gossip and friendly banter, but from the fact that, although some of her co-workers are three times her age, they treat her as a colleague and near-equal.

Admittedly, some of this respect may be because Le's family provide the room where the local alliance of silk weavers work together. Like many households in the neighbourhood, Le's family are self-employed textile workers, and it makes sense for such workers to club together to help each other out with rush orders and share the cost of light and heating if completing a job takes them late into the night – as nowadays it often does.

Sometimes Le thinks of the silk workers of Qi area as busy weaver ants, working unceasingly day and night as their busy looms churn out endless yards of silk for their wealthy and aristocratic customers. These customers trade silk between themselves for favours in the imperial court, dowries for their daughters, for bribes, and sometimes even – for clothing. Silk is a sort of unofficial currency, and transactions between the wealthy can involve thousands of rolls.

When Zhang Qian, the famous diplomat (d. 114 BC), went on a mission to the countries of Central Asia, he purchased goodwill by dispensing bolts of Chinese silk to the kings and warlords along his route. Everywhere the demand for silk keeps increasing, so it is little wonder that up and down the prefectures the empire is filled with the busy sound of weaving machines. The silk industry is booming, and skilled workers such as Le are much in demand – another reason why she is welcomed by the members of her small collective.

Still, it is wonderful to sit with the others in that small room off the family courtyard. Five looms packed in the small space feels very crowded, but for Le the closeness just makes the room all the more cosy and warm – something to be appreciated on a chilly May evening. There is also the jovial banter and jokes of a girls-only-night, and every now and then Le's mother pops into the room with warm drinks and words of encouragement (while surreptitiously checking on her daughter's progress through her workload).

No doubt Le's mother also misses the camaraderie of these evenings, but her increasingly arthritic hands can no longer operate the complex machinery of the loom. Le had been nagging her mother to allow her to work the looms ever since her eleventh birthday, but her mother always turned down her pleas. 'You are still too young and too small to operate the machine. You will be working soon enough, and then there will be days when you will be sick to death of the sound of the loom.'

Eventually, when Le turned fourteen, her mother was forced to step aside because of injury and allow Le to work with her sister-in-law, who patiently taught the trade to her eager student.

The sister-in-law told Le that she was fortunate to take up her new profession at a time when weavers were struggling to keep up with the demand for silk. The need to get more out of every worker has led to new and better machines and techniques. The latest machinery allows workers to power their machines with pedals while sitting, rather than alternately squatting and kneeling painfully at the loom as Le's grandmother had done. With their hands free, the workers can move the beams and handles of their complex looms to create patterns unknown to earlier generations. These new machines now dominate at both state-run factories and private workshops, enabling the production of silk rolls with wider frames and much more complicated designs.

A quick learner, Le soon became an experienced loom operator. She also quickly developed friendships with the other women in the weaving room, and as soon as she took charge of her own weaving machine she was treated by them as an adult, an independent worker to be given the respect due to one of her status.

Le is desperate to make sure that she does nothing to lower her standing in the eyes of the others. Carefully observing her fellow workers, she imitates their repetitive movements when operating the weaving machine, takes care to dress herself in the same style, and listens inquisitively to their conversations. She has quickly learned the jargon of a textile worker, such as the numeric short forms referring to the quantity of their products, and her speech is laden with the slang used exclusively within their own tight-knit female circle.

One of the things she has learned in the weaving room is how to make different kinds of small ornaments. Yesterday, she made a hemp rope and dyed it green with a herbal dye that a lady in the weaving room generously shared from her store of

Fossil casts of mulberry leaves, preserved in flood deposits 5 m below ground during the Western Han period

traditional knowledge. Le ties this rope to the basket that she tucks under her arm as she walks out of the house to replenish the supply of mulberry leaves.

Le's father had planted a stand of mulberry trees in front of their house when she was a small child. Like many of the changes shaking their world, these trees are an improvement on those used by previous generations. The new species has a shorter trunk and much denser canopy than the old trees, so there are more leaves to pick for the hungry silkworms, and the smaller tree makes it easier to pick them.

Some of Le's happiest childhood memories are linked to these trees. When the mulberries ripened in the summer she would climb the trees and stuff herself with the juicy fruit.

Once, when she was eight, she had collected berries in the pockets of the clothes her sister-in-law had just made for her. The juice left purple stains everywhere on the white fabric, and, not surprisingly, Le received a memorably long and very stern sermon from her mother. That was when Le learned that mulberries leave an indelible stain – in fact mulberries are among the many plants that silk workers use as dyes for their products.

'Did your mother wake you up too?' Le murmurs while rubbing her tired eyes. 'Can't they let us have a lie-in after last night?'

'No, my parents are still sleeping,' Tang replies, sounding firm but cool as usual. Naturally, Tang has remembered her duties all by herself. Sometimes Le thinks that Tang tries to be perfect just to annoy her. She notices that Tang's basket has a newly decorated handle and spontaneously exclaims, 'That is beautiful! What is it made of?'

'It is from a cassia tree. My father carved it yesterday and I painted the colour.' Tang seems quite pleased with herself.

'You will have to teach me how to do it later,' Le replies, slightly disappointed that her green hemp rope has gone apparently unnoticed by Tang. There is always an underlying competitive spirit between the two girls, and this has translated into their showing off colourful ornamental objects and other little home-made things. Naturally, Le's mother disapproves of this (mostly) friendly rivalry, but her father takes Le's side. 'Let them be, that's just how teenage girls are. Don't always be so critical.'

Deciding to ignore Tang for the present, Le turns her attention to the mulberry tree. All the usable leaves growing on the branches on the outer part of the canopy have been picked and only those growing inside the canopy are now available for harvesting. Despite the short trunk, Le can only reach these interior leaves with a hook that her father has made and customized to her height. She uses the hook to snag a suitable branch, then secures the branch to one arm with string while she strips off leaves with quick, practised movements.

She has not selected a good branch – many of the leaves are already mature and their tough fibrous texture won't be attractive to her silkworms. Ruefully, Le picks what leaves she can pick and irritably unties the string. The released branch bounces back, rustling the other branches and stirring awake the birds nesting in the canopy. These birds squawk in protest at the early morning assault and fly away.

Mixed in among the mulberry trees are some tung-oil trees. The blossoming season has passed and now the trees are laden with fruit seeds on their tall stems. Le's neighbour, the carpenter Wang, walks from his small hut to the tung-oil trees with a long pole in his hands. Seeing this, the easily distracted Le drops her half-filled basket and hook, and runs over to find out what Wang is doing.

In answer to the girl's query, Wang nods at the pole in his hands. He intends to use the long pole to bang the branches of the tung-oil tree and collect the seeds that he has jarred loose. These he will press to extract the oil. His daughter is getting married next month and he intends to make her an elegant cabinet that she can add to her trousseau. The oil will be used as a finishing touch to give the wood a beautiful sheen so that the carpenter's daughter will have a cabinet suitable for the home of a nobleman.

Wang smiles at Le and teases her gently. 'Surely your parents must be in a hurry to marry you off also? When do you want to become a bride yourself?'

Le blushes deeply as she shakes her head, but she keeps her thoughts to herself. She has decided that she is not going to get married, ever. Her ambition is to be the official in charge of dyes at the imperial Eastern Weaving Bureau, where she will be responsible for making beautifully coloured silk fabrics for the empress.

Actually, Wang knows this already and chuckles sympathetically as he hefts his pole and moves towards the stand of trees. Soon tung-oil seeds fall softly to the ground like snowflakes as Wang beats the branches and Le squats to help collect the seeds.

Wang wants to ask if Le has yet discovered that the imperial officials only hire male officers to supervise the dyes at the Eastern Bureau, but he can't stand the thought of the girl's face crumpling in disappointment should he be the first to break the unwelcome news. It would be cruel to shatter the girl's dream.

Instead, the carpenter changes his approach and asks Le how many colours she has learned how to dye. He knows that she won't be able to resist the opportunity to show off her newly acquired knowledge from the weaving room.

'I know the dyes for five colours and I have tried three kinds already,' Le tells him. She closes her eyes in concentration as she recites the strange names and exotic materials. 'Bluegrass (containing indigo) is for green, common madder (*Rubia cordifolia*) is for red, gardenia is for yellow, sericite is for white, and persimmon and holly leaves are for black.'

While Le is listing the dyes for different colours, Wang finishes picking up the seeds. Le is rather hoping that her display of expertise will encourage Wang to ask his daughter to try some dyes with her soon. After all, it is important that the daughter has the red colour just right before she dyes her wedding clothes. Before Wang can pick up on the hint, their conversation is interrupted.

'Le, are you finished yet?' Her mother's loud voice penetrates through the dense stand of trees. She knows full well that her daughter might have found something more interesting to do, and considers it her duty to make sure that Le does hers. With a reluctant sigh, Le begins to walk back towards the mulberry trees, and Wang gives her a sympathetic wave as she goes.

Tang (naturally) has remained at work and her basket now is almost overflowing with fresh leaves. She looks pointedly at Le's still half-empty basket, and then demonstrates that she can work and eavesdrop at the same time, for she now picks up the conversation Le was having with Wang.

'Do you know Le, the official textile bureau in our state is even larger than the one that works for the emperor and empress? My father told me. Can you imagine it? Thousands of workers working simultaneously in one place?'

Le shakes her head and her eyes grow wide as she wonders how that can be true. She can't imagine how large even the Eastern Weaving Bureau must be, let alone something larger. Her sister-in-law has told her all the details about the establishment and organization of the Eastern Bureau in Chang'an, which she had visited once in the days before she was married. She later told Le that the weaving room was illuminated by so many candles that it never got dark, and the sound reverberating from the weaving machines drowned out even the deafening chorus of summer cicadas during the hottest days of August.

Yet what Tang has said was true. Large as the factory in Chang'an might be, some textile producers have even bigger facilities. As with many other industries, Qi state, on the eastern coast, has perhaps the most developed textile industry in the Han Empire. Linzi City, the Qi state capital, boasts the so-called *sanfu* (three-clothing) factory, the most advanced operation in the business. It is a private company, yet the scale of its production can surpass that of state-owned factories.

'One day, we will be able to work in such big places,' Le replies with much more confidence than she actually feels. The hostility she occasionally harbours for Tang is gradually diminishing with the knowledge that they share a mutual interest and ambition. To keep the conversation going she asks, 'Tang, did you know that there is a goddess of silkworms?'

Le's new topic of conversation does not faze Tang in the slightest – instead, the other girl shrugs coolly and informs Le that, outside the Chang'an, in the western suburbs, there is a temple dedicated to the Goddess of Silk Worms. The empress was once in the habit of dedicating offerings and sacrifices at the temple every summer.

Tang has finished picking her leaves and, with a somewhat smug nod to Le, she walks away with her basket so full that leaves are almost spilling over the sides. Le pulls a branch down and starts stuffing her own basket while making a note to herself that she must find out more about the Goddess of Silk Worms. It's very annoying how Tang always seems to know more about everything than she does.

Le's mother calls a greeting as she emerges from the house, basket in hand. Le turns, expecting to be ordered to go and feed the silkworms as soon as she has finished collecting the leaves. Instead her mother gives Le a cheerful smile, not at all as irritated as she normally would be when Le is tardy with her allotted chores.

Her mother tells Le that she is planning to pick some elm tree seeds for lunch. The tasty dish made with these delicious seeds is certainly Le's favourite meal, but Le is not at all certain that her mother will be successful today, for the elm trees have seeded late this year. She pauses, and on reflection decides to let her mother discover this for herself.

Le sneaks between the trees like a rabbit and steps into her home with her basket full of mulberry leaves, curious and somewhat suspicious about the reason for her mother's unexpectedly good mood.

Female textile workers

The *Treatise of Food and Money* of the *Book of Han* says that the average working hours of a female textile worker could amount to nearly forty-five full working days per month because they often work extra hours or whole nights, compared to a male labourer's average of thirty days per month.

A middle-level agricultural household could expect an annual income of around 7,200 *qian* (Han money). An average adult female textile worker could contribute at least a further third to the family income by selling her labour and/or textile products. Apart from picking mulberry tree leaves and feeding the silkworms, textile production involved other arduous and complicated procedures. These included making the silk thread, reeling, spinning and weaving, as well as dying and other decorative processes.

辰 FOURTH HOUR OF THE DAY

(09.00–10.00: FIRST PART OF *SI*)

THE TOMB SCULPTOR TRAINS HIS APPRENTICES

I t should have been a leisurely morning setting out tools and finishing designs before starting work in the afternoon. Instead, the sun had barely risen higher than the poplar trees at the roadside before Dong and his assistants were hurrying to work.

They had expected to have plenty of time to complete the commission to carve bas-relief sculptures for the ancestral shrine and tomb of the Wang family. That was before a month's delay while everyone waited for the builders to finish the main structure of the tomb. Then, just to make things more complicated, the father of their employer fell seriously ill. Indeed, if popular rumour was to be believed, the old man might not last the month. This had led to his son pushing the builders to finish their work in a hurry. Dong now has to complete the tomb carvings to a very tight schedule, for whether the father survives or not his family intend to dedicate the tomb at the end of the month, and the event cannot be postponed.

The Wang family are well known locally and their affairs are a common topic of discussion and rumour. The family patriarch passed away a few years ago and the family business is now in the hands of the third generation. The new head of the clan is the eldest grandson of the founding patriarch; an impressively elegant and self-assured man in his mid-thirties. Dong has met him several times when presenting sketches of the images and structures he had designed for the family monument and he was impressed not only by the young man's politeness and sophistication, but also by his detailed knowledge of the auspicious meanings and symbols in the designs for the proposed bas-relief carvings.

Usually, when Dong is preparing such a commission, he helps the employer select and design the images, and then he sketches the rough drafts himself before the carving begins. But the Wang family knew exactly what images and designs they wanted for the structure, which will serve as both an ancestral shrine and a family tomb.

Just a generation ago, the family would have been content with a more basic tomb, crudely carved in the style of the era. But the new wave of prosperity has particularly enriched the merchant class, and a new professional class – the skilled stonemason – has developed to meet their need for increasingly elegant and expensive memorials. A top stonemason can gain national repute, and there is a constant quest for new styles and techniques that will impress clients. Some stonemasons who feel they have much to offer might travel hundreds of miles to the capital in the hope of displaying their skills on an imperial project. Others travel from client to client, leaving lasting memorials to their skill at sites across the country.

Dong has hopes of joining this elite group, and he had been looking forward to this job as an opportunity to showcase the

EASTERN HAN DYNASTY TOMB PANEL WITH A RELIEF OF FIGURES UNDER
A PAVILION. THE LARGER FIGURE ON THE LEFT IS XIWANGMU, WHO
PLAYED A MAJOR ROLE IN HAN FUNERARY BELIEFS, SECOND CENTURY AD

skills of himself and his assistants. He was planning to use his
best styles and his most elaborate designs, to impress not just
the Wang family, but others who might see his work. Who
knows? Maybe this tomb might lead to a contract to fashion
the tomb of a royal courtier, one of those remote, elaborately
carved tombs situated deep in the mountains, packed with the
treasures that accompany the dead nobles into the afterlife. Yet
the delays in building the Wang family tomb seemed to have
brought these plans to nothing.

Now, still breathing hard after the morning walk to the
work site, Dong turns to the wall in front of him, shaking his
head in frustration. Instead of a smooth surface waiting for the
stonemason's carvings to bring life to the stone, the wall is a botch
job, completed in haste with whatever materials were on hand
when the stone the builders had ordered did not arrive in time.

Not only were the builders forced to use white sandstone, but they had mixed this with whatever other stone blocks they could dress in a hurry. Dong does not really blame the builders for the sandstone, for given the lack of any other material, what else could they have done? But he is annoyed that they seem to have inserted the blocks at random when building them into the wall.

The result is an untidy mixed-coloured surface of stone, each block with different textures and qualities. When Dong first saw what the builders had done, he had racked his brain to figure out some way to carve the beautiful design of his employer's sketches into this random assortment. He knows now that the end result is an unsatisfactory compromise, but shrugs his shoulders with resignation – he can only do his best.

The white sandstone has been a nightmare – and the end result will be far from an enduring testimonial to Dong's skill. His clients seem to believe that stone lasts forever, immune to the effects of wind and rain. Good-quality granite may do so perhaps, but white sandstone sucks moisture from the air like a sponge – and when saturated it crumbles away. Fine carving is wasted on such a surface, and Dong is gloomily aware that his work will have vanished within a decade.

Given the poor-quality sandstone and the need for a consistent style of carving and polishing across the different rock surfaces, Dong has decided to use the simplistic sculpting style that has recently become popular in the area around the Chang'an capital. He is basing his redesign on the classic stone sculptures that he first saw when he visited the area as a young apprentice. He sighs as he remembers those exciting days, when stonemasonry first rose from a crude mechanical skill to be considered a form of craftsmanship comparable to the making of lacquers, bronze work and fine ceramics. If only the builders appreciated this when preparing the raw material for his craft!

Dong's two assistants are also his nephews, but as Dong does not have any sons of his own, he considers the two as almost his own children. Wistfully, Dong remembers the relaxed work schedule that he had originally envisioned and wishes they could have kept to that. It had seemed a great opportunity to further train his nephews in their craft. But now he cannot afford to have them make any mistakes, because there simply will not be enough time to correct them.

Much of the carving has been done, and the nearer the job gets to completion, the more care they have to take to avoid any damage. Dong reminds himself to warn the lads that they have to be gentle when using their iron chisels on the white sandstone, for that stone is quite brittle. It is also hard and coarse-grained, which has made it difficult to carve the delicate lines of the more elaborate images. Even polishing the finished work is going to be tricky.

Dong puts the toolbag on the floor and assigns tasks to his apprentices. The older nephew is less skilled than his brother, for all that he has been at the job longer. Still, he is steady and conscientious and will complete whatever job he is assigned. Dong sets him to finishing the polish on the green stone surfaces that the lad had started yesterday. This green stone takes up much of the wall on the right. It is fine-grained limestone, which means that it will take a polish well. However, that same fine grain makes the stone that much harder. Polishing it is a time-consuming job, especially as Dong insists that the finished stone should be smooth as leather and bright as a mirror in the morning sun.

Though the style Dong has chosen for this tomb is simple, it is far from unsophisticated. It actually takes a lot of imagination to conceive work in so natural-looking a style and considerable skill to make the transition from concept to reality. The craftsman must understand the texture of the stone and adapt the style to his material. Particularly crucial is how well the sculptor is able to incorporate into the design of his work the veins of different minerals running through the stone.

This simplistic style is far from the complicated carving styles favoured by sculptors in Dong's native Yiping (formerly called Donghai) Prefecture, but it is becoming popular in Chang'an after it was imported from a neighbouring prefecture further east. Stonemasons are a highly mobile breed, and the best artists travel considerable distances to fulfil lucrative contracts. They bring with them new styles and ideas that are picked up by local craftsmen so that their art mixes and blends with time and changing tastes.

While his oldest nephew starts polishing the green limestone Dong walks towards the younger nephew, who is arranging their iron tools on the floor. Of the two of them, Dong thinks the younger one has the better combination of artistic ability and skilful hands. The youth will be his ideal successor – not that Dong has any intention of telling him so just yet.

'I have explained the many carving techniques to you already. Now let's try some out.' Dong pats the nephew's shoulder in recognition of a good job at organizing the tools. Two axes, two hammers, a number of chisels with different-sized blades, two saws, a few small drills and several knives are tidily laid out from left to right. The challenges of the stone surface have forced Dong to use all his tools and skills. Multiple techniques have been called into play, including simple intaglio line carving for concave and convex surfaces, shallow bas-relief carving, high bas-relief carving and openwork carving.

Stone-relief carving techniques

Stone-relief tombs emerged during the middle-late Western Han period and became extremely popular later, as well as during the Xinmang era and the Eastern Han period, especially around Nanyang, northern Shaanxi and Shandong. In typical Eastern Han-period stone-relief tombs, these carvings were often combined and positioned on orderly partitioned spaces to represent an idealized 'tripartite universe' consisting of the heavenly domain, the domain of the immortals and the mundane world of ordinary humans. Archaeological evidence suggests that groups of sculptors specialized in stone carving in areas such as Gaoping, of south-west Shandong.

The next job requires simple intaglio line carving. On a small side wall beneath the roof are three slabs of stone on which Dong has sketched figures, animals and some geometric patterns. The black ink stands out clearly on the polished surface, so now Dong picks up a knife and chisel and walks closer to the stone. With his thumb he establishes that the blade of his knife is not sharp enough to do the job alone, so he decides to carve the initial lines using the knife together with a chisel. He says as much as he passes the knife for his nephew to examine. He remarks that the blacksmith in town produces steel knives that keep a keen edge even after repeated use – but such blades are rare and prohibitively expensive.

Taking back the knife, Dong presses it into the stonework and slowly traces along the black ink lines. 'Always hold the knife steady and press as hard as you can while keeping an even pressure,' Dong tells his apprentice as he finishes a long line with the knife. He passes it to the boy, who is watching him closely, and then he reaches for the hammer and chisel.

Dong holds the chisel almost perpendicular to the stone wall and starts to hammer. He slowly creates a tiny groove along the line he has just carved. 'Always hold the chisel skewed, but at a slight angle. Hammer gently and try not to peel any stone debris away.' The nephew nods his head; he is well used to receiving instructions that start with 'always'.

Even with the simple intaglio technique to incise the lines into the stone, there are nevertheless many small things that could go wrong at this point. Despite this Dong lets his younger nephew take over – although he keeps a close watch on his progress. Grudgingly, the stonemason has to admit to himself that his nephew is doing quite well. His carved lines look neat and professional.

'Steady, always steady, always follow the sketched lines exactly.' The young man is carving the curl of an elephant's trunk. Dong is so focused on supervising the work that he does not realize his older nephew is standing behind them and watching.

'What is that? Is that a hook or something?' The older nephew laughs as the trunk slowly takes shape. Dong doesn't laugh, for he knows that these curly lines are not easy to cut – doing them well takes an exact combination of pressure from the wrist and a sharp eye for detail. To allow the younger nephew to concentrate on his assigned task Dong irritably shoos the older apprentice away.

Swiftly and competently the younger nephew carves out the rest of the elephant; trunk, legs and back. It is actually not the first time the younger nephew has carved a whole design by himself and it seems that he has nearly mastered the simple intaglio technique. Dong is pleased but he does not say so.

Indeed, every time the young man lifts up his chisel Dong is right there, rattling instructions as if the nephew is a complete novice. An apprentice cannot get enough training – eventually doing things just right must become second nature.

Dong decides to let the lad carve the remaining two small figures on his own. 'Always hold your breath and be careful with the edges,' he repeats unnecessarily and then walks over to check the polished stones, although he knows that the older nephew will work conscientiously until lunchtime when he will have completed this routine, laborious job.

Dong touches the stone surface and studies the gaps between the slabs as he shakes his head in silent complaint. The spaces between the stones are supposed to be firmly sealed with lime, but how carelessly the work has been done! Some slabs are not even mortared properly into place and might drop out at any moment. *Aargh*, those builders!

The Wang family wants the image of their mansion carved onto this wall. While Dong has never been inside their house, he was shown the plan in their design. He cannot remember where he put the sketch, which had been drawn on a piece of leather, so instead he draws a rough outline on the floor with a piece of chalk. Then he turns to the wall.

The striations on the sandstone slabs at the top of the wall seem to resemble ridges, so these can become the tile lines of the roof. Dong and his apprentices can even repeat the same design on the slab beneath to create a pattern representing a multi-storey building. Then, when they have chiselled the background out, the roof will appear nicely as a shallow bas-relief. Dong picks up a chisel and hammer and demonstrates to his apprentice what he wants done, adding the oft-repeated and unnecessary warning that the chisel must always be held almost parallel to the stone.

Standing back, Dong puts one hand to his chin as he surveys the work in progress. There, on the limestone on the lower half of the wall that his nephew is polishing, they can carve detailed lines that represent the gates, windows and other features of the house. They will paint the roofs black, and the gates and windows red. Overall, he is rather pleased with this plan, although it does feel rather sparse.

Usually a much wider variety of images and patterns are carved on the walls and roofs of such tombs. The main themes include cosmological and heavenly features, auspicious beasts such as unicorns and other imaginary animals, or perhaps scenes from daily life such as dancing, feasting and farming. Sometimes religious figures might be portrayed, scenes from legend, or even occasional erotic elements.

More animals should be depicted in the present design, Dong feels, preferably auspicious beasts bringing good fortune. However, the head of the Wang family is a hard-headed businessman rather than a mystic, and his chosen design reflects his uncluttered yet elegant approach.

Once they have finished here, they will move on to complete other parts of the ancestral shrine. Dong is getting curious about what further challenges this will bring.

THE SALT WORKER HARVESTS BRINE

The Duke of Huan asks, 'So how to rule the state?'

Master Guan answers, 'The only strategy is to manage the mountain and the sea.'

The Duke of Huan asks, 'What is managing the mountain and the sea?'

Master Guan answers, 'A kingdom of the sea should take its policy on salt taxation seriously.'

Haiwang (*Kingdom Based on the Sea*),
Volume of Guanzi (Master Guan)

It is already past mid-morning when Gao leaves the brine lake. It is not laziness that dictated his late start, but the tides. Gao and his fellow workers had to wait until the waves receded and the hot sun had started to evaporate the seawater off the brine pan where he works. For a nineteen-year-old, the young man trudging across the beach is already remarkably disillusioned with life.

Salt! The white gold from the sea. As a boy, Gao used to marvel that the magic of the sun could turn bland seawater into beautiful salt crystals. And in turn those salt crystals could transform basic ingredients into delicious dishes for the table. His grandfather used to salt fish and then smoke it, and the fish so prepared would be the main ingredient of his grandmother's renowned fish-and-rice recipe.

Gao's grandparents have now passed away, and he very much misses them, as he also misses the tiny fishing village that he was in such a hurry to leave behind when he went to work at the salt pans. Given how eager he was to get out and explore the larger world, it is a poor consolation that he had no choice but to leave anyway. He is the first in his family not to be a fisherman, but fishing in these waters is a risky business. Catches are good, but the waters are hazardous.

Last year his father and older brother were well out to sea when they were caught by a storm. Skilled sailing and a great deal of luck allowed the pair to save their nets and gear, but the strong currents and waves, combined with the force with which they finally beached, almost tore their boat apart. Having to borrow money off the neighbours for a new boat was a chastening experience for Gao's father, and it made him determined never again to put the family's financial eggs into a single basket.

As a fisherman he had never heard the term 'diversification of financial risk' but Gao's father well understood the principle. He was an authoritarian character who required his oldest son to live under his roof even though the 'boy' was now a grown man, married, with a child of his own. It only takes two men to operate their fishing boat, so young Gao was available to supplement the family income in other ways. At the fish market it was rumoured that the local salt producers were looking for labour, so Gao was told to pack his belongings and move to his new place of work.

The salt producers run a private operation, and therefore business is somewhat precarious. It is not that there is no market for their product – there is no one so rich or poor that they can do without salt. In fact that is the problem. Salt is a form of currency; everyone needs it and those who produce or sell this essential commodity hold the key to wealth and power. Initially, the government was content to let private producers bring their salt to market while getting fat on the taxes they levied. But from the start, salt production has been a controversial business. Even with the hefty taxes extracted by the government, salt industry tycoons accumulated huge wealth and resources, to the extent that they threatened the political and financial stability of the empire.

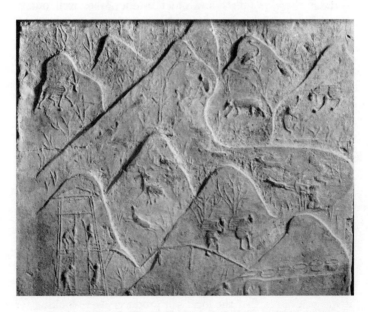

EASTERN HAN STONE RELIEF SHOWING PEOPLE WORKING IN SALT
MINES WITH PANS FOR EVAPORATION SHOWN IN THE FOREGROUND

Not that these tycoons allowed any of their vast wealth to trickle down to the labourers they employed. The drive for profits was so intense that government officials investigating the exploitation of salt workers were shocked. (And given the conditions endured by those labourers who work directly for the empire, anything that can shock an imperial official must be very bad indeed.)

Add misery at the bottom to overweening power at the top, and the situation was ripe for trouble. In one of the wealthiest salt-producing districts, 'king' Liu Bi gained popular acclaim by abolishing taxes on farming land. Eventually, Liu became the leader of the 'Seven Kings Riot' – a turbulent affair that remains one of the empire's most bruising memories. This led to the decision to take salt production out of private hands.

Salt and iron in the Qi state

The book *Guanzi* (Master Guan) is a collection of philosophical and political treatises, attributed to the Spring-and-Autumn-period philosopher and politician Guan Zhong (*c.* 720–645 BC) who served as chancellor in the Qi state of East China. Through Guan's series of economic reforms, including the establishment of state monopoly of salt and iron production, Qi became one of the most powerful vassal states during the Spring-and-Autumn period. In Guanzi, Guan Zhong articulated his philosophy of statecraft on various political, economic and fiscal aspects. In the *Haiwang* volume, Guan Zhong provided a detailed economic account of how to manage the mountain and the sea, through which a kingdom based on the sea could be founded.

In theory, this should have worked well. Salt production was supervised by the Imperial Privy Treasurer, who eventually shifted the bulk of his responsibilities to the *Dasinong* (Minister in charge of agriculture). Government officials keep an eye on the market, and since salt does not decay, they can use the state's huge salt reserves to stabilize prices, selling salt cheaply when it becomes costly, and restocking their reserves when the price drops.

However, government officials like to look good to their masters. They do this by making their departments as productive as possible. With a state monopoly and no competition, prices rose even as the quality of salt fell, and the conditions of the workers deteriorated once more. There's no easy remedy to the situation, as many arms of government have become dependent on these short-term profits and strongly resist demands for reform by merchants and other businessmen.

By now the state has started to monopolize everything it can make a profit from (even mountains are taxable), but there is a limit. Some reckless souls had always taken the risk of producing salt privately, and recently they expanded their operations to meet the demand for a lower-priced better-quality product. The imperial authorities have come to realize that they must allow what they can't prevent, and they have permitted a small degree of competition from private producers. But whether production is state or private, the work remains very hard. Those who go into the state production are often young men who would otherwise be homeless vagrants. Those in the private sector are prepared to endure the appalling conditions for the chance to earn high wages and a share in the final profits.

Gao is one of the latter breed. He puts up with the conditions because of the money it brings his family, but any idea of the romance of salt harvesting has long fallen by the wayside. It is brutally hard. That sun that transforms the salt does not feel so magical any more. Like the other workers who labour all day beneath its blazing heat, Gao now considers the sun a curse. His skin is coated with salt spray and flayed by the sun until it resembles cracked tree bark. It is difficult to open his puffed eyes fully, and his hair always feels damp and gritty. Gao has a gloomy suspicion that he smells much worse than the dead fish-heads that lie in his father's refuse pit.

Behind Gao are the crude huts of his temporary home. In theory, he does not have to live there, because a worker can construct his own quarters if he is so inclined. The problem is water. There are no streams or rivers on this part of the coast, so fresh water comes from very deep wells. It is normal that, after many failures, the deep freshwater aquifers can be reached for drinkable water in the region's saline groundwater. So wells are dug by the state, or by wealthy landowners. An individual or poor household would not have the means to dig very deep wells that would provide fresh water.

Also, the owners of the salt workshop have two carers who are tasked with keeping the workers fed and provided with drinking water. This owes less to compassion than the fact that men who are cooking and fetching their own water are less productive where it matters most – in harvesting salt. So Gao stays at the huts and drinks the foul-smelling water. This morning, even though he knows it is going make him drink even more, he added a pinch of salt to the water. This not only ameliorates the taste, but is necessary for his health. Salt workers on this coast are allowed a level of salt only permitted elsewhere to soldiers working in the harshest conditions in the empire. (The equivalent of 30 g per day.)

Over the coming hours, while Gao is working to crystallize salt, the same substance will be draining from his body as sweat. Keeping his body sodium levels up is one of the first lessons Gao learned when he arrived here. The second was whenever possible to avoid the curse of that burning sun.

Now Gao squints across the overly bright water as he looks at the levels on the brine lake. This is an artificial shallow bay built in the intertidal zone specifically to trap seawater. Yesterday, on the bed of that lake Gao helped to lay out an inch-thick layer of ash, pressing it hard into the lake bottom so that the ash would absorb more salt.

Today, they have hurried to begin the harvest before the tide rises, for the lake will be flooded again by mid-afternoon. He and two of his colleagues have spent the past hour scraping clay and ash off the lake bed and piling it at the lakeside. Sometimes they harvest the clay one day and extract the salt the next. Recently, though, they have been taking advantage of a small rise in salt prices and have taken on enough temporary workers to perform both operations simultaneously. It's a chance to make some extra money, and that is what everyone is here for.

Gao sweeps up the sun-dried mush from the lake floor, while a co-worker picks up the piles he has accumulated. This worker carried the mixture of ash, salt and clay to the boiling location set up on the narrow path on a corner overlooking the lake. (Another boiling location is set up further down the beach to deal with the overflow.) Having cleared his area, Gao picks up an iron chisel to prise off the stuck lumps that he was unable to sweep up. As he bends down, a sudden gust of wind blows up the dust from the swept ground into his face and eyes. The powdered mix of salt and clay causes instant pain and blindness, and Gao sits down hard, groping for a cloth and his water bottle. Even now that he has bathed his eyes, they are red and sore. There's an itchy feeling to them that he knows will not go away for the rest of the morning.

The still-receding tide reveals a pit that Gao had dug yesterday when the tide was lowest. He had put down a layer of bamboo, a layer of reed matting, and a layer of fine, clean sand. Seawater salt is abundant but elusive stuff. Brine lakes are one way to trap it, but they don't work everywhere and are large-scale operations. Pits can be dug by one man and give a good yield of salt-rich brine.

Gao looks up the beach to where several of his co-workers are at work kindling a fire under a large black iron pan. Despite their best efforts at conservation, all the trees have been stripped from the area behind the sand dunes and fed to the insatiable fires. One can travel further inland towards the mountains and get timber from there, but that takes time. Time that can be spent in the more profitable business of making salt. Instead, Gao and his co-workers take turns gathering dry grass. Grass is terrible fuel, and burns wastefully fast, but it also burns hot and yields abundant ash for spreading on the lakebed.

Reckoning the pan will be ready by the time he gets there, Gao collects two buckets and fills them with brine from his pit. Setting down one bucket by the fire, he pours the other slowly into the pan, where the brine hits the hot metal with a satisfying hiss. As the second bucket is added, the pan settles a bit deeper into the hot stones that comprise their crude oven. Whitish bubbles begin to float to the surface from the middle of the pan and quickly spiral out to the edge as the salt starts to crystallize. Gao nods to a co-worker with satisfaction. That was quick, which means the brine must be saturated with salt.

Gao works to accelerate the crystallization still further by adding more fuel to the fire, which is burning more strongly now as the coastal winds blow over it. The wind is a mixed blessing that rapidly becomes a curse, for the iron pan and open fire radiate heat – as though the blazing sun were not hot enough. Gao and the other workers are forced to move back and upwind to avoid the heat and caustic fumes blowing off the pan.

During that brief break, Gao watches the Kong family at work further down the beach. Like the other temporary labourers, the Kongs are paid according to the salt they produce, and because the family live locally, every one of them with time to spare pitches in. The two younger children are tending the fire, while an older son drags a bucket of brine from the family pit. Kong's wife is walking slowly and carefully across the beach. With each footstep she sinks ankle deep in the damp sand, for the woman is bowed down by a load of timber. Gao marvels at the determination that has taken her from the woodlands beyond the sand dunes all the way to the beach while carrying that load.

At the edge of the brine lakes, a bird perches atop a dune and serenades them with a stream of harmonious twitters. Gao takes a moment to imagine the scene through an outsider's eyes. He sees a picturesque beach beside a blue ocean. The mountains rear green and grey in the background and the sound of birdsong floats through the air. He shakes his head. You have to work here to understand how hard it is.

'Gao! Get back here,' a co-worker shouts. He is needed back at the pan, where the seawater is quickly evaporating in clouds of stinking fumes while the last of the moisture sizzles off, leaving the precipitated salt crystals. At first, it all looks like a mess of white sand, rustling softly as it dries. Left to itself, the minerals within it would set dry like white concrete, so Gao stirs the mix gently, all the while using a small scoop to deposit the newly harvested salt into a bucket.

'The gift of the sea.' Gao dips a wetted fingertip into the salt and tastes it. It's good stuff, and he enjoys a moment of relief and celebration. His pit has given him a good yield, even though a large part of it will go to the workshop owners, and the taxman will take much of what is left. Yet Gao is not tempted to produce more than his allowance. On a co-worker's foot an ulcerated wound is still healing. The man was caught producing salt without authorization and for weeks he had a heavy iron chain cuffed to his ankle as punishment. His relief when freed told Gao all he needs to know about the efficacy of the punishment.

A call floats over the sand. 'Gao, they're ready at the lake!' The seawater has evaporated enough for a fresh stretch of lake bottom to be swept, so Gao stands, stretching his cramped limbs. His moment of relaxation is over already. He thinks, 'Here we go again.'

午 SIXTH HOUR OF THE DAY
(11.00–12.00: FIRST PART OF *WU*)

THE PRIEST ARGUES WITH A FRIEND

Fan Chi asked what constituted wisdom. The Master said,
'To give oneself earnestly to the duties due to men, and, while
respecting spiritual beings, to keep aloof from them, this may
be called wisdom.'

The *Yongye* chapter, *Analects of Confucius*

The priest Gongsun had a strange dream last night. A Qilin unicorn with a cloudy halo above its head approached and stopped in front of a tree, the trunk of which reached almost to the sky. With its mouth, the unicorn plucked a golden twig from the tree and then disappeared into the forest.

Such dreams leave the priest feeling unsettled. He suspects that the dreams are related to his fascination with the many different temples and religious rites in his region. He likes to visit these when he can, and enjoys the music, dedicatory offerings and varied rituals that are offered to honour a wide variety of gods and goddesses.

Gongsun reflects wryly that in his royal palace, the emperor also is probably having strange dreams of unicorns and divine trees. The emperor (Emperor Wang Mang 45 BC–AD 23) is something of a radical, and his reforms have overturned the more staid religious practices of previous generations, creating a somewhat febrile atmosphere in the temples, which Gongsun finds at once fascinating and disturbing.

It does not help that Gongsun is sophisticated enough to know that the emperor's religiosity stems not from true devotion but from political calculation. As the founder of a new dynasty, Emperor Wang Mang's legitimacy is constantly questioned, but fortunately the ruler is also a brilliant Confucian scholar. He has used this knowledge to manipulate rituals and rites to persuade his largely Confucian officials that he has every right to preside over the state.

To show his respect for tradition the emperor has carefully maintained the ancestral temples of Western Han emperors inside Chang'an city, and, more importantly, he has built a dozen new temples outside the city to enshrine his own ancestors and thus strengthen his dynastic claims. Wang Mang carefully observes the Zhou rites, one of the stricter forms of religion, and is punctilious in his religious observance. This mixture of innovation and tradition at the top cannot help but be reflected in the observance and practice of religion among the emperor's subjects.

Thus, the ramifications of imperial religious policy affect even the humdrum life of the priest of a small rural temple near Chang'an, for Gongsun's life is dictated by the calendar of religious events and rituals that take place throughout the year at the temple. Yet, unlike the emperor, Gongsun's devotion to religion has no ulterior motive. It is simply that service to the gods and goddesses and ancestral spirits is more important to him than everything else, and he is quite content that every other aspect of his life is subordinate to that service.

Furthermore, Gongsun very much enjoys his work and is proud of his role in the village. Not only does he look after his temple; he also organizes events for the local farmers and their families so that they have an opportunity to socialize and meet kinsfolk scattered around the community – no easy thing to manage otherwise during the busy farming season.

The only thing that constantly concerns him is finding the funds to maintain the temple and support the many events it holds. While state temples are directly funded by the government, local temples are expected to support themselves. If the harvest has been good, local farmers willingly contribute grain, animals and other practical support to the temple. In lean years, the farmers barely have enough to support themselves and their families, let alone give offerings elsewhere. Ironically, it is also in the midst of these bad years that the farmers and their loved ones flock to the temple for comfort and support and demand more ceremonies with which to beseech the gods for better weather.

Fortunately, during the first half of this year, the weather has been clement and the seasonal ceremonies have gone off without a hitch. The feast of Sheji, the God of Land and a Hundred Grains, took place in February, and attracted a pleasingly large crowd. As might be expected in a farming community, this celebration was one of the biggest events of the year. Almost the entire local population gathered at the temple, where abundant food, including a whole sheep and pig, were offered to the god and shared by the local people.

Nothing pleases Gongsun more than to overhear delighted participants at such events comment on how much they are enjoying themselves. Gongsun has known for years almost everyone who attends and regards it as a part of his duties to see that they are happy and entertained. But time flies when things are going smoothly, and already preparations for autumn worship are just around the corner. Gongsun remarks as much to a friend, one of the local elders who is visiting.

'How much food gets consumed during ceremonies such as these?' the local elder enquires.

The question seems to be one of harmless curiosity, but Gongsun knows better, and bristles at the implication that the village food supply is being squandered. He takes it all the more personally because that is simply not the case. Everyone receives their share of the bounty, with the meat being distributed in equal portions to the aged folk of the village, and boiled grain given to the women and children. And, of course, there is always plenty of wine to go around for everyone. Yes, indeed a lot of food is consumed, but Gongsun is very sensitive about suggestions that any of it is wasted.

The elder holds up his hands placatingly. 'Would you please relax. I wasn't criticizing you – just wondering how we can keep depleting our resources in this way. One day, the granary will be empty, the sheep and pigs will all be eaten, and there will be nothing but dust in the wine jar – and then what will we do? I once attended a Sheji ceremony in the west where all they had to offer to the god was one chicken, one peck of broomcorn millet, one peck of foxtail millet, two pecks of wine and half a litre of salt. Can you imagine that?'

Well, of course Gongsun can imagine that – in fact he worries about it all the time. Yet he feels strongly that cutting back on offerings to the gods can only be counter-productive – the gods will certainly not make the crops abundant if they are afterwards denied their fair share of the harvest. Perhaps this might be a good moment to lobby the visiting elder for his support for a plan that Gongsun keeps urging the villagers to adopt. Gongsun knows his friend well and has often discussed temple business with him, so the elder is better informed than most villagers about the practicalities of running and maintaining a rural temple. Also, the elder is revered in the community and an important voice among the villagers.

Recently, some communities have started to collect money for their seasonal religious gatherings. The problem is that a cash payment would be high – a burden even for government officials, and an almost intolerable one for farmers. So Gongsun wants locals to take turns working the village's communal land, with designated individuals responsible for things like sowing and harvesting. The sale of the crops thus produced would go a long way towards covering the expense of temple ceremonies. That way the temple can finally stop living from hand to mouth and move on to something more stable.

Just as they are talking about labourers, two volunteers from the village walk in. The priest looks at them blankly for a moment before he remembers that these are volunteers whom he had asked yesterday to help him prepare offerings. Excusing himself from the elder, Gongsun takes the pair directly to the kitchen, where a bowl of wheat grain waits on a low table beside a small pile of melons. The men are regulars at the temple and are familiar with the set-up of the kitchen, so without any delay they get started on firing up the kitchen stove, washing the wheat and preparing the melons. This leaves the priest standing at the doorway feeling slightly redundant in his own kitchen, so after a minute he leaves the helpers to their work and goes to rejoin his guest.

The local senior is still there, standing by the paintings on the walls. Gongsun tells him of the dreams he has been having lately.

'Do you think the gods are trying to tell me something?'

At first the elder does not answer, choosing instead to contemplate one of the paintings, which shows a figure with a large, open mouth from which is billowing smoke or clouds.

Two winged men stand on either side of this central figure, looking rather like cosmological retainers.

This is the God of Winds, and Gongsun knows why the elder has chosen to stand before this particular painting. Once, during a spell of dry weather, the two men had seen visiting wizards dressed in wonderfully extravagant outfits performing colourful, exotic magic for the Wind God while dancers dressed as monsters beat a drum as they tried to evoke the God of Lightning and bring down the rain. These *Wu-xi* witches and wizards are considered important mediums through whom mortals can communicate with the heavenly gods. Revered by villagers, they are also one of the most influential groups in the imperial court, and involved in prayer, divination, astrology and medical activities.

Naturally, the elder had been unimpressed by the whole event, commenting that while he had nothing against god-fearing piety, it did worry him greatly when people became obsessed with religious ceremony to the point that they forgot other vital tasks. The gods help people, certainly, but they do not personally dig ditches, clear irrigation channels or construct public buildings.

It's an old argument, and now Gongsun reconsiders asking his friend to bring his plan to the villagers. He knows that the elder disapproves of ostentatious and costly demonstrations of religiosity, especially wizard and witch performances such as that one they saw performed for the Wind God. Gongsun glances over at two cattle horns and three cattle tails hung on the opposite side of the hall. These are used in wizardly performances, but out of deference to the elder's strongly expressed opinions, the instruments have not been taken from the wall for a long time.

The elder finally comes to his point: Gongsun's dreams, he says, aren't just about the gods, but also about people. Perhaps the gods are trying to tell their priest that some of his celebrations have become rather too sumptuous of late. Gongsun's locals are beginning to like his lavish events for their own sake, and it might be that in his dreams the gods are suggesting that the point of the ceremonies is supposed to be worship of the divine, not enjoyment of an extravagant party.

Gongsun counters that there is nothing wrong with worshipping and appeasing the gods, but he agrees that those who focus on the celebration have forgotten the true meaning behind the event. 'We should be more conscious about tailoring the ceremony to fit the occasion – I completely agree. We should instruct people about the right things to do, and guide them in doing them, certainly, but that does not at all mean we should dismiss religious ceremonies altogether.'

One of the helpers has walked out of the kitchen and has been leaning quietly against the door while listening to the debate. Now he interjects that personally he enjoys watching performances and listening to music during religious ceremonies. There's not enough music lately, says the volunteer. He then gives an account of a ritual music performance that he recently saw outside Chang'an. Boys and girls had stood in rows singing in chorus until they were hidden by the encroaching dusk.

'Ever since then I have wanted my son to have the chance to be moved by the beauty of those sweet songs.'

There's hardly a religious ritual in the district that Gongsun has not attended, and he immediately recognizes the volunteer's description as the ceremonial singing of 'The Four Seasons Songs'. He tells the helper that nineteen other song cycles are performed during religious ceremonies in rural Chang'an. All were written by Sima Xiangru, the famous poet, writer and politician who pioneered the *yuefu* style of poetry.

Many of Sima's songs are odes to the Sheji god, and by way of demonstration the priest sings the first verse of one of these songs. When Gongsun has finished, the volunteer simply looks at him in bewilderment, for the complex literary lines of the song are beautiful, but also incomprehensible to an untrained ear.

The elder, on the other hand, has enjoyed both the song and Gongsun's rendering of it. 'Now that,' he observes, 'is beautiful, appropriate and educational. We should teach all our local children to sing songs of this sort.'

Gongsun snorts derisively, wondering if the elder is out of his mind. Having just complained about the resources being expended on religious ceremonies, he now wants to set up singing classes for children? Politely, he begins to explain that hiring a teacher and setting aside a lesson area is something the temple simply cannot afford.

From the corner of his eye Gongsun notices that the volunteer has become a bit crestfallen. If the volunteer was hoping that his son might get a temple education of some description, he might as well know now that his wish is simply unrealistic. The priest wonders if this is what has motivated the volunteer to help around the temple and whether, now that his hopes have been dashed, he will ever return again.

The other helper emerges from the kitchen to announce that the bowl is filled with boiled wheat grain and the melons are cut. 'Is there anything else that needs to be done?'

Gongsun thanks the helper and informs both men that people have dropped off donations of firewood and charcoal and left them placed randomly outside the hall. It would be very helpful if the men could pile the firewood in one corner and place the charcoal in a large basket that Gongsun has designated for this purpose.

One helper asks, 'Why do you need all this firewood and charcoal – are you going to perform a *liao* smoke sacrifice?'

Gongsun laughs and shakes his head, amused by the idea of staging so grand an event. *Liao* smoke sacrifices occur only when royalty or the very wealthy decide to make a large bonfire and dedicate ornaments of jade or other precious materials to the flames. These sacrifices sometimes take place in May, October, or occasionally in March. It would probably be sacrilege, or at the very least disrespectful to the gods, for someone to set up a *liao* smoke sacrifice without having jade or other expensive goods to offer.

Instead, Gongsun explains that he is merely planning ahead for the autumn, when a bonfire will fit well with some of the harvest festival celebrations he is planning. Seeing the elder once again shaking his head in disapproval at the priest's prodigal waste of resources, Gongsun pointedly abandons his guest to join the volunteers in loading charcoal into the baskets. As they work, the second volunteer asks, 'Gongsun, my neighbour renovated his kitchen stove the other day, and offered a sheep to the Kitchen God when he was done. His grandson is serving in the army, and my neighbour thought that the Kitchen God will protect him. Is that what I should do? As you know, my son is also joining the army soon.'

'The Kitchen God watches over everything in this earthly world and should be worshipped with deep reverence. If you can afford it, you certainly should also renovate your kitchen stove – though you must be sure to consult me so that we can select an auspicious day for this. When your son goes away, let him keep a handful of earth from the kitchen hearth so that he will become homesick and want to return to his family when he can.'

Gongsun goes on to explain in more detail about worshipping the Kitchen God. Even the other helper, who thinks he knows everything, is now listening carefully and occasionally nodding his head in agreement.

After holding his peace for as long as he can, the elder finally feels forced to intervene. 'People should never arrogate the rites by over-stretching their finances with sacrifices that do not match their social status,' he states flatly. Gongsun reflects that Emperor Wang Mang would certainly agree – both emperor and elder are of the opinion that the primary function of religious rites is to maintain the social order.

Gongsun shrugs, for he and the elder have been over this same argument so many times that there is no point in going over it again. Instead, he decides to usher his unhelpful guest off the premises and begin preparing his midday meal.

Temples and sacrifices

The Western Han inherited many Qin period (221–207 BC) gods as well as temples. The early Western Han Emperor Gao called back wizards who had served in the Qin court, and reinstated them in several high government positions. These wizards brought their folk beliefs into the Han court and many new gods were created.

The number of official temples rose throughout the Western Han period, to more than 1,700 during Wang Mang's reign. Gods worshipped in these temples included the gods of mountains and rivers, gods of the sun, the moon and stars, gods of winds, rain and all kinds of ancestral gods. These temples consumed an enormous amount of state resources – under the Emperor Xin Liu (27 BC–1 BC) approximately 37,000 sacrifices were made annually, each involving huge amounts of food, wine and other materials.

午 SEVENTH HOUR OF THE DAY

(12.00–13.00: SECOND PART OF *WU*)

THE WARDEN OF THE BEACON TOWER COLLECTS HAY

The black ramie coat is not Chen's favourite. There's nothing wrong with ramie, which is a plant fibre woven to make basic garments, but the colour is wrong. Properly speaking, only soldiers should wear black, but in Chen's isolated outpost one takes whatever clothing is on offer at the market. The good old days had long gone when local officials would supplement his government clothing allowance, so now Chen must make do with his annual issue of one coat, one unlined tunic and a pair of trousers – all of which wear out long before the replacements are due.

And his boots! He was given these boots when he started the job forty years ago. Even though he now wears them only on special occasions, they are pretty much worn through. Mostly he wears hemp slip-on shoes, and even these his wife has repaired so often that they now have more replacement fabric than original material. Given his workload, Chen wears out the flimsy hemp shoes fast. Already one toe is starting to poke through the last set of repairs.

Chen sighs and picks up an iron sickle as he goes through the courtyard and out of the tower gate. He has a few moments between other jobs, and he plans to spend the remainder of his day cutting hay in the meadow beyond the fort. The fort is one *li* (about 500 m) away, four walls enclosing a 10-m tower. Soldiers, looking like busy beetles in their armour, march down the stairs of the main building to join others who are already at drill on the parched grass near the main gate. There have been reports of Hun raiders nearby, and the soldiers are on high alert.

THE KIZILGAH BEACON TOWER NEAR KUCHA MARKS
A CHINESE GARRISON POINT ON THE SILK ROAD

The guards under the tiled arch of the west gate of the fort stir as Chen approaches, and he watches them warily. Lately, their raillery has passed into outright abuse. Last time he went by, a guard had shouted, 'Chen, how much have you pocketed today? Remember to keep putting up the price of lamb!'

This was a reference to the warden of Tower Twenty, who had told his soldiers to sell some lamb for forty-five *qian* more than the usual price. The buyer had reported that warden for profiteering and he had been fired from his post. This had created a local scandal, not because the money involved was a substantial amount, but precisely because it was not. For a trifling sum the man had lost his job, his title and his reputation. While the general opinion was that the warden of Tower Twenty had been unworthy of his rank, Chen could understand the man's struggles. There are few ways to make money on the frontier, and when your funds run out, what is a man to do?

The guards on the west gate are at it again. 'Hey, Chen! You are wearing black. Have you been demoted to being a common soldier?' Chen grins back politely while the guard runs his hand down his own coat, which is of fine wool with a cross-woven pattern. 'This thing cost me 1,500 *qian*, can you believe it? Times are tough!'

As he hurries by, Chen wonders who bribed the guard with that coat and what the bribe was for. Sensing Chen's disdain, the guard shouts after him, 'Your boss, the *duwei*, has just taken a piss, so you had better check what you are supposed to do about it.'

This is partly a dig at Chen's position in the administrative hierarchy. Chen ranks as a *gongcheng*, the eighth of twelve bureaucratic positions. This is not bad, and plenty of Chen's colleagues in the rich central plains have ways to milk money from their rank. But here on the arid frontier, Chen is in the worst of all situations. He has responsibility without much power, and precious few benefits to accompany his rank.

He does not earn much either. A tower station is expected to be self-sufficient, though no one has explained to Chen how he is to achieve this. The Han government supplies military necessities such as weapons, but everything else has to come out of Chen's own allowance, which, shockingly, is less than that given to the three soldiers under his command.

The problem is that most tower wardens are wealthy men who take the job for the prestige that goes with the rank. Chen has no other income but his allowance, and he cannot afford to embellish his tower as wealthy men do. He lives in dread of his rank being stripped away, leaving him and his son with no status at all, so he tries hard to impress his superiors with his diligence. This is why he now hurries to cut hay in what should be his free time before lunch.

His position is actually safer than Chen realizes, for those tower wardens who take the job for the title and status prefer employment in areas other than outside a desolated frontier fort that the Huns might attack at any time. Rumours have been flying around concerning what the Huns might be up to, and just this morning Chen took the chance to interrogate the postman when he arrived with a batch of decrees from the regional government.

These decrees warned him to prepare for Hun attacks. He and other tower wardens were to shore up their defences by whatever means necessary. There would be inspections and punishments for any warden found wanting. Soldiers must practise diligently at their archery. (Again, the warden is responsible for any soldiers who fail to reach a satisfactory standard.) Horses must be kept in their stables, and, naturally, the warden is responsible if any are found grazing outside the tower.

Chen is not too worried about his preparedness. His three soldiers have been training hard for the upcoming *qiushe* competition in September. Last year, their average score was a very satisfactory eight out of ten. One of his men had actually won an archery award. Even Chen's ten-year-old son (his older son died on campaign six years ago) is learning horsemanship and archery alongside the soldiers. The horses are well looked after, so he has nothing to fear on that account either.

The Huns have their own festivals, and in the past they would refrain from so much as sharpening their knives and polishing their saddles until these were complete. Yet the postman reckons things are different this year.

Recently, Han and Hun had ostensibly come to a high-level diplomatic agreement. A Han princess had been married to the Hun *chanyu* (a rank the equivalent of a senior general). She took with her bundles of the finest silk, stocks of wine and sacks of rice, partly as a dowry and partly as tribute, yet still this has not stopped the Huns from raiding. Chen has seen the smoke signals from other towers. This smoke is short-lived, meaning that, for the present at least, the raiders are few and disorganized. Towers Thirteen to Eighteen were badly damaged, less by the enemy than by their own chaotic contingency plans. The official in charge was punished – as much for his efforts to cover up what had happened as for the debacle itself.

One of the reasons Chen is now gathering hay in the meadow is that he does not want his own plans to be found wanting. He is a small cog in an enormous machine, but the smoke from his tower might at some time pass along information crucial to the military situation along the whole frontier, and Chen wants to be prepared.

It is his job to immediately understand the meaning of the smoke from signal fires in the towers around him and to pass on the information as the situation demands. The carefully prepared system means that Chen needs to memorize different categories of fuel – for in the signalling system, grass smoke and the smoke from different types of wood all contain their own meaning. These meanings are supposed to be a state secret, but Chen is reasonably sure that keen observation has allowed the Huns to work it out by now.

One quickly extinguished beacon fire is the lowest category, signalling the approach of fewer than ten raiders. Then the alerts go up until they reach a stage-five alert – a non-stop fire that signals that a force of more than a thousand men are not only marching on the tower but actually attacking it. This system of signals is the only way to get information quickly across the wastes of the north-west frontier, and the authorities are merciless with those who fail at this essential duty.

The warden of Tower Twenty-Two was a close friend of Chen. Once, after a desultory Hun raid, that friend had left his signal fire burning while the other towers had extinguished their smoke in a timely fashion. Chen could only watch in despair as the forgotten fire from Tower Twenty-Two had finally burned out of its own accord. The Han representative on the border had not been amused at having to mobilize his army on a false alarm. When the tower warden had been unable to provide a satisfactory excuse for his negligence, he was sentenced to fifty strokes with a wooden paddle. This was a severe punishment, for the paddle is heavy and designed to cripple. Chen's friend has been bedridden and partly paralysed ever since.

Thinking over all these matters has made cutting the hay light work, so now Chen stands, straightens his back and regards the result of his efforts with satisfaction. On the arid frontier, the little lake beside which he has been working is almost a miracle of nature. True, the water is brackish, but it makes up for this by supplying the fort and tower with salt, and the saltwater grasses at the lakeside make excellent thatch. Those grasses are on the other side of the lake, though – the sweeter grass he has cut here will be fodder for the horses, now that it is too dangerous for them to go out to pasture.

Chen stacks the grass, and decides he will now stop for his midday meal and come back tomorrow with a horse to bring the hay to the tower. Now he needs to get back to see how the soldiers have done with the repairs. The tower is old and needs constant maintenance to keep it from becoming run-down. Chen needs to keep the place in excellent condition, not least because he can't afford to pay the inspector to overlook any deficiencies. Last time the inspector had rolled his eyes at the crumbling plaster, clearly expecting a bribe. He had gone away disappointed, and Chen had known that the place needed to be flawless by the time of the next inspection. He needs the money that this corrupt fellow expects to be paid off with, and so the inspector must be given no excuse to make difficulties.

The tower has a wide rectangular base, but it is not that high. Indeed, until Chen put in a staircase, people climbed to the top by a rope. The walls are made of logs padded with reeds held in place by layers of plaster. Depending on the clay and the season of the repairs, the adobe wall is in places blueish, reddish or white. Over the decades Chen has repaired the tower time and again, but there is always more to do. When he was younger and more energetic, Chen had done all the repairs himself, but now he feels no shame at delegating the soldiers to assist him.

Before he set off to cut hay, he had left the soldiers with grass and clay that he had prepared beforehand, along with a wooden trowel. Iron is in short supply in these parts (which is one reason why Chen and the iron sickle had gone together to the lake) so the soldiers have to make do with a wooden trowel. Over the years Chen has become proficient at both making and using wooden tools, and he reckons the soldiers can also become as skilled as he. By now, if the soldiers have been working diligently, the new surface should already be smooth and drying in the wind and midday sun.

This leaves the men free for the next job, which will take them 5 *li* to the other side of their tower. Two poplar trees had been standing dead there by the riverside ever since they were killed by the drought last autumn. Chen had been keeping an eye on them, because though the government is meant to supply essential timber, more often he had to get lumber for himself. Anyway, these trees would be used for repairing columns damaged by fire last winter. Even though Chen constantly reminds the soldiers and his son that fire is as much a danger to the tower as the Huns, inevitably accidents happen. When they do, of course, the authorities hold Chen responsible, so making good the damage is up to him.

A few days ago they cut down the trees, and Chen marvelled at his good fortune, for the trunks were in excellent condition. They say that poplar trees live for three thousand years, stand for three thousand more after that, and do not decay for another three thousand years thereafter. Chen won't be around in nine thousand years to find out if this is an exaggeration, but certainly the rugged poplar matches the mentality of the border folk, hence their use of it for building rather than firewood. (Though Chen has plans to come back and grub up the stumps for the latter purpose.)

One tree has already become a supporting column in the stables, and the second time around Chen is hoping to avoid the drama involved in getting that first trunk back to the tower.

The weight of the wood had been too much for their cart, and a wheel had shattered in the first pothole they hit. While Chen and an older soldier tried to patch up the wheel, a younger soldier had run to the tower to bring an extra horse and a rope. They used this rope to temporarily bind the damaged spokes while apprehensively eyeing the gathering clouds that suggested a sandstorm was on the way.

Sandstorms are so common that they are a major complication when it comes to sending smoke signals. In fact this is one reason why the tower has horses – so that a mounted messenger can carry news when smoke signals cannot. No one wants to be that messenger, because the best place to be in a sandstorm is safely indoors. Certainly, one does not want to be choking on dust while pulling a wobbly cart as it lurches down a rutted road, while behind it two very unhappy horses pull a heavy log through the billowing sand.

It was worth the horses' hard labour however, now that the log column makes their stable more solid and secure. Some minor repairs to the stable roof, Chen decides, and the building should easily pass the next inspection. The stables are the first thing that gets checked, because horses are highly valued assets. Sometimes Chen feels that the government places the welfare of the horses above that of humans, since people like Chen and the soldiers are more easily replaced. Chen likes the horses and wants them to have a tidy stable, but he does not agree with the government's position.

In fact, as he nears the tower, Chen is pondering whether it might not be better to take one of the horses and go back to get more hay right away. He has now ascertained that the grass in the lakeside meadow is lush and abundant. He and the soldiers working together can bring in a whole cartful, and then tomorrow they will go out to get the remaining poplar.

Suddenly there is a shout from the tower. 'Fires up!'

Chen breaks into a run and rushes into the courtyard. Across the desert he can see that smoke is already rising from other signal towers. He yells to the soldiers to get their flags up and the horses readied while their own fire is ignited. There will be no time for hay-making today. Instead they must face the Huns.

未 EIGHTH HOUR OF THE DAY

(13.00–14.00: THE FIRST PART OF *WEI*)

THE GRANARY KEEPER IS INSPECTED

The Jingshi granary is not a single building – it is more of a mini-city of granaries. The complex takes up hundreds of thousands of square metres with many large warehouses, each surrounded by smaller warehouses. Each of the large warehouses can store up to 10,000 cu. m of grain. When fully stocked, the granary city has the capacity to store over a million *dan* of grain. (A *dan* is 30–32 kg.)

Hong is responsible for warehouses Nos 1 and 2, which are located right in the heart of the granary city. In fact, at 1,660 sq. m, Warehouse No. 1 is the largest warehouse in the whole complex. His is an important job, because the grain in the warehouses feeds the army and other workers of the emperor. When Hong started work at the granary, they told him, 'These warehouses are the actual heart of our country. Without them the entire kingdom would crumble away in no time.' Now, after years of experience have taught him what the granaries mean to the empire, Hong has come to believe this completely.

The importance of the granaries is one reason why Hong is currently being even more careful than usual with the deposit of grain supplies. According to reports, the main Han army has been marching towards the granary for months, and Hong wants to be prepared for whatever might happen. Hong's fellow villager Bai works in the army, but he could tell Hong only a little about the army's plans.

'What do I know? We're just nobodies who do as we are told. It looks like the soldiers will be here for a long time, though. Tents have been erected, stoves built, and we are told that soon winter clothing and boots will be handed out too.' Hong is not happy about this, both because the army will literally eat through his grain reserves, and because he was hoping that Bai could carry some messages to his wife back home in the village, but it seems as though that is not going to happen soon.

Hong's family does not live far from the granary, but they are still too far for him to visit as often as he would like, especially now that he has extra responsibilities. He came to the granaries a few years ago, as a relatively humble *Cangzuo* (assistant keeper of the warehouse), and while in that relatively junior position he was able to go home every couple of months and help his wife with the farm. But thereafter, the bureaucratic hierarchy underwent some dramatic changes.

First, the *Cangjian* (inspector of the granary) was arrested for corruption. Since the warehouses cannot run properly without someone in that position, the government quickly replaced him. Having removed one corrupt official, the government was careful not to substitute another and the granary staff quickly discovered that their new boss is honest, conscientious and ruthlessly efficient. When he first arrived, the replacement *Cangjian* collected the account books, and spent much of his time checking the records, and then checking them again.

This led to the exposure of more scams and corruption – for after all, few things are more easily converted into cash than grain – and to another round of firings and consequent promotions – including Hong's – to fill the newly created vacancies. Hong stepped into the shoes of his former boss and moved from assistant manager to being the manager of Warehouses No. 1 and No. 2. He rather welcomes the extra responsibilities that come with his new job, but these responsibilities do make it hard for him to leave his post.

The inspector has warned that if the warehouses are not maintained to his exacting standards, punishments will follow. For example, warehouse keepers have been warned that if they allow birds and rodents to get in and eat the stored grain, criminal prosecution will follow – something that makes Hong reluctant to leave his warehouse in the care of subordinates, even for a quick trip home.

To start his afternoon, Hong is finishing the paperwork for the new batch of grain that has just arrived. Yesterday at dusk, Hong had been waiting beside the heavy wooden gates to personally oversee the grain entering Warehouse No. 1, and after the last cart had been unloaded, he had personally locked the gates in the presence of two granary guards.

At the time he had quickly jotted down the type and volume of grain on a bamboo slip, and this afternoon he wants to double-check these figures and add more information, which the assistant of the *Dasinong* (Grand Minister of Agriculture) will need when the records are audited. 'Eighty-three *dan* of millet, delivered from east,' he finishes, and adds his name and those of the two guards present. 'In total, 1,652 *dan* of millet, May.' This is the net amount of grain entering his warehouses this month. Hong is about to calculate the gross throughput of grain and the net surplus of the past two months when a messenger from the *Dasinong*'s assistant arrives. Hong is ordered to drop everything and report to the gate – his warehouse is about to be inspected.

Hong is unruffled by the surprise inspection, which he has been expecting for some time now. The *Dasinong*'s assistant runs regular checks on the warehouses under his charge and another of these checks is about due. Hong reminds himself that his records are honest and his conscience is clear, but the intimidating scrutiny of the *Dasinong*'s assistant always makes him lose his nerve. His records will be painstakingly checked against those from his last inspection and audit, and the assistant will be very thorough in his investigations.

The inspector may also look for signs of damp, for despite the relatively high elevation of the Jingshi warehouse complex, it is relatively close to the canal, so damp is always an issue. There is also mould, which is a particular obsession for Hong, not only for professional reasons but because, having seen so much starvation in his native village, he passionately believes that letting good grain go to rot amounts to a moral offence against humanity. If traces of damp or mould are found in his warehouse, Hong will be harder on himself than even the inspector would be.

His obsession has made Hong very familiar with damp-proofing technologies, and he constantly harangues his colleagues about the vital importance of keeping the air circulating. 'The grain needs to breathe' is his unofficial catchphrase. Usually the grain is stored on suspended wooden floors inside the warehouse. This space (up to 80–90 cm) between the wooden floors and the ground allows good ventilation, and air convection is further helped by mesh-like holes and small windows between the thick walls. There are also double eaves built on to the edge of the high ceiling to keep rain water out of the warehouse.

As he walks to the granary doors to meet the inspectors, Hong keeps an eye on the early afternoon sunlight filtering through the mesh below the eaves. There's a kind of moth which reproduces rapidly in damp conditions, and Hong knows that if he sees one of these creatures fluttering in the sunbeams then he has a hidden problem developing somewhere.

Hong has ideas that he wants to present to his superiors, and is wondering if this inspection might be a good time to do this. While he appreciates that the current design of the warehouses permits good insulation, moderate sunlight and proper ventilation, there is always room for improvement. For example, he once spoke to a soldier from the Shu region in the south-west of the empire. There, lighter construction materials such as bamboo are used to build granaries. Not only are bamboo walls cheap and the material abundant, but such walls allow for excellent ventilation. Hong does not believe that it is feasible for the Jingshi granary city to switch entirely to bamboo, but with some improvement and modification, he thinks they could try these lighter materials on parts of the roof and walls.

Hong opens the gates of the warehouse and the *Dasinong*'s assistant and his entourage step inside. As he left his office, Hong had picked up the records for the three months since his last inspection, and now he passes these to one of the staff members of the *Dasinong*'s assistant. While these are being inspected, he talks the assistant through the numbers as they walk through the warehouse.

The building is currently only at one-third of capacity, but it feels quite overwhelmingly full already. The sweet aroma of grain mixed with the gritty taste of chaff floats to greet them as they approach the mountains of grain. Hong points out the relatively small mountain on the far left.

'That is from March. The net surplus of that month was small. The weather was not good and there were several days that the canal was completely non-functional. Usage that month was also rather high. There were days as well when several carts of grains were disbursed to feed horses when their fodder ran low. The net total for that month comes to 899 *dan*.' The *Dasinong's* assistant wordlessly turns to the member of his entourage who holds the records. He looks at the man enquiringly, and his assistant takes a scroll of bamboo records from his pocket. Evidently the *Dasinong's* assistant wants to cross-check Hong's report with other records – the guards keep their own tally, and the inspector is probably using their reports.

The *Dasinong's* assistant says nothing while the records are being unrolled on the floor. Hong walks to the grain pile in the middle and continues, 'The warehouse was replenished in April when canal transportation returned to normal. The quality of grain in some of these batches was quite high.'

The *Dasinong's* assistant asks where the grain came from, and there is a pause as Hong checks his own records and replies, 'Mostly from the mausoleum counties near the capital.' He bends and, with both hands cupped together, scoops up some of the grain and pours it into the hands of the *Dasinong's* assistant. The assistant selects a few grains, crushes them between his heavy fingers and smells the pulverized bits. The man smiles slightly. 'Those counties have fertile lands, and always produce high-quality grain as long as the weather permits.' It is quite a relief to see the *Dasinong's* assistant's serious face finally break into a smile, if only for a moment.

The official is being meticulously thorough, but Hong does not hold this against him – in fact, he thoroughly approves. He takes his work very seriously and likes it when others do the same. The management and defence of the Jingshi granary complex has to be particularly rigorous due to its strategic location at Chang'an, the capital.

These warehouses are enormously important to the empire and, because of this, the site has seen several hundred years of bloodshed as Han rebels and state armies have fought repeatedly over the mountains of grain stored here all year round. In any war, the granary complex is an irresistible strategic objective, for the army that controls the granary has an overwhelming advantage. Grain feeds the soldiers, and can also buy the loyalty of towns whose fields have been devastated and allies looking to feed their own troops and people while the enemy starves.

As the celebrated Li Yiji (268–203 BC) once observed, 'A king's life depends upon the people; and the people's life depends upon food.' At the time, Li was persuading Liu Bang, the founding emperor of the Han dynasty, to take back control of the Aocang granary. Liu Bang's subsequent success encouraged later Han governments to dedicate enormous effort to the building of state granaries and putting these massive warehouses behind carefully planned defensive structures.

The Jingshi granary complex is an excellent example, for it sits at the confluence of the Yellow and Wei Rivers, isolated by steep cliffs on the other sides. Grain flows into the warehouses through an imperial transportation system that has been dramatically improved in recent years. Just the construction of the Caoqu canal alone has dramatically increased food transportation from several hundred thousand *dan* a few generations ago to around six million *dan* in 110–105 BC.

The Jingshi granary is managed by a special office set up by the Han court called the *Chuansikong* (Ministry of Shipbuilding). Though it is only a county-level ministry, it oversees and manages a local ship-building department, the granary complex and canal transportation in the region. The granary also, unsurprisingly, is well guarded, and Hong wants to discuss this as well with the *Dasinong*'s assistant if he gets the chance.

He feels strongly that the warehouses should be more strictly separated from the military encampment and the inevitable civilian settlement that has grown up alongside it. Humans living too near Hong's precious grain pollute the water and leave food waste that encourages scavengers, which then raid his stores. He has reported this problem several times to his superiors, but nothing has happened. With gloomy pessimism Hong reckons that the issue will be ignored by the authorities until something disastrous happens, and by then it will be too late.

Recently, Hong has been getting more and more worried about the warehouses catching fire. The warehouses he looks after are often downwind of the cooking area of the military camp. Let just a tiny ember from those open fires fly into the dry, flammable mountains of grain and the subsequent blaze might wipe out the whole granary city. Hong searches for a diplomatic way to suggest that the *Dasinong*'s assistant visit the artificial ponds not far from the granary city where water is stored for this type of emergency. Really, he should see for himself how inadequate those reserves would be in the event of a raging, all-consuming fire.

The man cross-checking the records has finished his calculations and is rolling up the scrolls on the floor. Hong knows from previous visits that this man is actually a skilled forensic accountant and even while Hong was giving his verbal report the accountant was probably calculating the figures in his mind. After Hong reports a net gain of 1,851 *dan* for the warehouse in April, the accountant takes out a tablet and scribbles down the figures. It is a relief to see this being done, for if the accountant is now recording new data it means that Hong has – more or less – passed the audit. Nevertheless, he will not completely relax until every one of his reports has been matched with the remaining stocks of grain.

The *Dasinong*'s assistant quickly checks the reserves stored in the right-hand corner of the warehouse and appears to be satisfied. Evidently the volume of grain matches Hong's records. The cross-checks with the guards' records also show no discrepancy, so with luck all that remains is the final document to be signed and sealed before the inspection is over.

They wait for the accountant to finish writing, and then they step outside the building. However, the *Dasinong*'s assistant has one more surprise in store. In the space behind the warehouse gates a bronze measuring device is stored. After checking that the device is in its proper place, the *Dasinong*'s assistant turns back to speak to the accountant.

Hong waits with trepidation as the accountant goes to a bag he left in the courtyard when he arrived and, like a magician performing a trick, pulls from the bag an almost identical measuring device. In sudden realization, Hong grasps that the *Dasinong*'s assistant intends to check whether the warehouse measuring device has been tampered with. Some sneaky warehouse keepers shrink the size of a standard measuring device and embezzle the difference when giving out rations to soldiers, low-rank officers, and others whom they reckon incapable of complaining. Fortunately, Hong has never even thought about this, let alone done anything of the sort.

The accountant takes the shining bronze container, which Hong assumes holds the standard volume of one *dou* (peck) of grain. He pours the contents into Hong's measuring device and everyone watches with interest to see if any grain is left over.

A BRONZE MEASURING CUP WITH A DRAGON HEAD HANDLE

If there is something left in the standard vase after Hong's device has been filled, then Hong's measure of grain is smaller than the official standard. Even knowing that his conscience is clear, Hong watches nervously until he sees that the measure of grain in his device exactly matches that used by the accountant.

The *Dasinong*'s assistant and his entourage finally step out of the warehouse with Hong still in attendance. With its contents now assessed and checked, the warehouse can be sealed, so Hong locks the gates under the watchful gaze of the assistant. He takes a tablet of greyish clay and sticks this into the small gap between the two gates, then presses the two ends of the clay tablet together and stamps it with his own seal. The accountant then stamps the clay to add the *Dasinong*'s assistant's seal, so that Hong's and the assistant's titles are clearly visible on the clay.

This is a very important security measure widely used across the empire. After the tablet dries, no one can open the gates without breaking the tablet, and if the sealed tablet is replaced, Hong will notice this immediately. Next to the main gates are two small single-leaf doors. These are for Hong's own use, convenient when he needs quick access to the warehouse for odd jobs. Hong now seals the gap between the single-leaf door on the left and the wall with a further clay tablet.

Outside the main gates of the warehouse is a rounded stone on the pavement. This is there so that arrivals can wipe off dirt stuck on their shoes before they enter the warehouse. Hong cleans the stone regularly, but this morning he was too busy with the grain shipment that arrived yesterday, and now the gaps between the stone pebbles are caked with dirt. Fortunately, the *Dasinong*'s assistant and his entourage have already walked away, so it seems that Hong has got away with this minor oversight.

Nevertheless, he grabs a broom and quickly starts sweeping out the dirt. From one side of Warehouse No. 1, a soldier runs towards him. Earlier, the man had come to draw grain for the military kitchen and Hong had told the soldier to wait outside. The soldier must have understood that business had been delayed by the *Dasinong*'s assistant's unexpected visit, but he wants Hong's attention now. Hong puts down his broom, walks to the soldier and takes out the keys for Warehouse No. 2. Still much work remains to be done before Hong's day is complete.

THE COURIER
APPROACHES HIS
DESTINATION

I t has so far been a difficult first day back at work for Zheng. After riding for hours, an ache in his thigh reminds him that his leg is not quite fully healed from its recent break, and he worries that he might have come back to work too soon. While he was recuperating he tried to help out around the house as best he could, helping to grind grain and doing minor household repairs. Because Zheng is a courier, his family gets a tax exemption for the one hectare of land that they farm. This saves some costs and helps to cover daily expenses, but Zheng is not paid while he is not working. So, every day, Zheng tested his leg, eager to get back and start earning a salary – and also (though he is not prepared to admit this even to himself) to escape from spending all day in a confined farmhouse with his extended family.

Zheng has spent much of the day today on horseback, for his journey is too far and his leg still too weak for him to run with messages. When he is on the top of his game, Zheng the runner well merits his nickname of '*kuai ma*', which means 'fast horse', although Zheng well knows that he is better than that – over medium and long distances a human runner can actually go faster than a horse, especially over rough or hilly terrain.

It was in fact a horse that had let Zheng down on the last occasion he had carried a message. The message was important – a drainage dyke had collapsed in heavy rains and the local authorities needed to be informed quickly if they were to prevent widespread flooding. However, after slogging through rain and mud for 50 *li* (around 24 km) Zheng's horse had become exhausted, and the courier had impatiently decided to abandon the animal and finish the journey on foot.

The heavy rain and poor visibility were not an issue, for after working as the local courier for three years, Zheng's brain is imprinted with a living map of the countryside. He intimately knows the valley corridors, the fords across the creeks, the short-cuts through dense forests, and every other detail of the landscape of Baling county where he works. All the more humiliating, then, that he stepped on a slippery pebble while crossing a minor creek in the rain and broke his leg while falling.

This morning Zheng had reined his horse up to study the place where he had fallen that rainy night. He reflects that in a way he had been fortunate, for while he was trying to push his way through the mud with his arms, a soldier had seen him from the road. The man had brought him to safety on a cart taken from the same local postal station that had taken over the delivery of Zheng's urgent message. (Fortunately, this close to the capital, there is always a post office nearby.)

The capital, Zheng's destination today, is still several hours away, for yet again he has a message for the department of the interior. This message was the first thing he'd seen when he got into work that morning. He had fed his horse and ridden it to the station, where he was warmly welcomed back by the manager of the postal station. On entering the office, from professional habit he looked immediately at the low table on the left-hand side of the room, where documents that need to be delivered are normally placed.

A fast runner from boyhood, Zheng reckoned that he was always destined to be a courier, so his family had skimped on certain parts of his education. As a result, he is barely literate, but he recognized the characters on the bamboo document on the very top of the pile as '*bao zai*' (safeguarding from disaster). The stamped seal on the document further informed him that this was an important message. Zheng was trying so hard to read the other characters on the seal that he did not realize the postal manager had followed him into the room. 'Zheng, there was a widespread hailstorm in the eastern part of the county. Local farmers need to be warned of the unusual weather so that they can take precautions.'

So it is to be another trip to the city, and despite the fact that Zheng's horse today is clopping peacefully downhill and that the mid-afternoon sun tells him he is making good time,

A SILVER SEAL WITH A TURTLE MOUNTED ON TOP. THE INSCRIPTION
UNDERNEATH REVEALS IT BELONGED TO A HAN-PERIOD GENERAL

Zheng is still cautious. The only official punishment he has ever suffered in his career as a courier was the result of a message for the city. He had been charged with getting a census report to the department of the interior, and his miserable government-supplied horse had stubbornly refused to wade through the waters of a shallow but fast-moving creek. In the end Zheng had to complete the journey on foot, and even his famed running speed had not been enough to prevent him from arriving late.

The punishment was fifty strokes with a bamboo cane, administered by the manager of his postal station. This was not a severe punishment as such things go, not least because it was administered by a man sympathetic to his predicament, but the humiliation still rankled. One good thing did come out of the debacle, though – and that is the horse on top of which Zheng now sits.

Partly because Zheng's failure also reflected badly on him, the county governor – who must have heard about his case from the postal manager – has recently developed something of an obsession with speed and efficiency. The problem is that government-supplied horses are not particularly compatible with either of these objectives. Naturally, the army gets the pick of government horses, and those left for the postal service are old, useless or former cart-horses commandeered or purchased from local farmers. (Not that cart-horses are bad in themselves – quite often, high-ranking officials or their aristocratic friends make use of post-station horses and find it useful to have trained animals to pull their carriages; but this does not help with the speedy delivery of the mail.)

Instead, the county governor, influenced by the post-station manager, has started to experiment with hiring private horses for the postmen. This also sidesteps the entire bureaucratic process of using a government horse for deliveries. State-owned horses kept in postal stations require the users to present authenticated recommendation letters, and thereafter the user's status, purpose, issuing organization and other information have to be painstakingly recorded in a ledger. Furthermore, many of those users are high-status individuals who usually consider that their needs come before those of a mere courier, so often the mail has to wait until the horses are returned.

Now, rented horses are available to picked couriers, and Zheng is among the first beneficiaries of the new policy. Evidently, whoever had completed the delivery of his letter had done so with some kind words about Zheng's dedication in attempting to get the message through. As a result, he was given this horse for his personal use once he had recovered from his broken leg.

So far, the horse has been impressive, making excellent time over the ground outside the post office, wet though it was after the recent rain. The north–south road that cuts through the fields has been expanded recently, and is now surfaced with a mix of roof-tile shards, pebbles and hard-packed yellow earth that spills rainwater into the ditches on each side of the road. On his new steed, Zheng gets through this part of the journey much faster than usual, the only delay being the unusually busy road around one of the small local towns. Here, Zheng has to force his horse through workers pushing heavy, weather-beaten carts loaded with goods for the local market.

There are also crowds of migrants, for the changing economic conditions have set large parts of the population on the move. Some of those clogging the road are economic migrants heading into the towns to take advantage of urban prosperity, while others are refugees from natural disasters that have driven them from their farms. To control the latter, the state has long set up a rudimentary welfare system, handing out food to those dispossessed by disasters. This is not so much altruism as a desire to avoid having large groups of desperate and hungry people wandering about and disrupting the harmonious running of the rest of the country.

Of course, the increased bureaucracy involved in the welfare system has generated more paperwork, and the need for more couriers to move that paperwork around. Over the past turbulent century, the state has learned the hard way that the central government needs to be promptly informed of disasters and civil disturbances in outlying areas, and it needs a way to get orders as soon as possible to those in the afflicted region. The postal service has grown to meet the need for the bureaucracy to become ever more interconnected, with decrees and orders rapidly disseminated to distant outposts, while those outposts send to the centre reports of disasters, civil unrest and harvests good and bad.

So postal stations have been cropping up around the country like mushrooms after rain, clustering most thickly around the capital, but spreading far and fast, so that nowhere, no matter how remote, is now without a postal station. Sometimes, in more isolated areas, a dozen or so households would form an alliance to set up a post station responsible for the dispatch of government documents and urgent mail. At other times, the postal service would rotate, with each family sparing one man at a time to carry the mail. Over time, more competent and trustworthy people (among whom Zheng counts himself) became the area's permanent or semi-permanent couriers. While an injured courier might work on the family farm, as Zheng has been doing over the past few months, the usual convention was that a permanent courier should not be involved in any other business that could compromise his position.

A multi-tiered postal system

You postal stations were placed every 10 to 30 *li* throughout the empire. The main functions of *you* postal stations included delivering mail, reporting local affairs to higher-level officials, and announcing public notices, as well as being hostels for civil servants passing by.

Zhi postal stations were established every 10 *li* or so, sometimes as replacements for the *you* postal stations. Some scholars think that *yi* stations were functionally similar to *you* and *zhi* stations, while others suggest that the character *yi* referred not to the post house but to the means of transmitting information – e.g. by mounted courier.

Ting stations were at a much higher density across the empire, especially in rural areas. Some figures suggest that there were almost 30,000 *ting* stations set up during the reign of Emperor Ping (1 BC–AD 6). The multi-functional *ting* stations delivered official documents and transmitted information, and sometimes provided basic accommodation and meals for travellers and civil servants.

After he had struggled through the market-day crowds, Zheng felt that the day was getting on, so he had decided to see what the horse could do. He gently encouraged his new steed to ever-greater speeds as they cut across the gently rolling plateau toward the zigzag pass over the mountains.

This pass is a crucial link connecting Zheng's region with the rest of the county, so the government has invested considerable effort and expense in maintaining it. As a courier, Zheng has a keen appreciation of the condition of local roads, though he is occasionally baffled by the decisions of those who build and maintain them. For example, about an hour ago, after turning a sharp corner, Zheng discovered that the road on the second-tier cliff has now been inexplicably widened to almost 30 m across. The steep slopes on either side are protected by multiple layers of pounded earth, but the recent heavy rainfall has still scoured several small gullies into them and the drainage ditches are already half filled with eroded earth and gravel.

Zheng had shaken his head at this apparent waste of effort, especially as further up the pass conditions were much worse, and the road there could have done with some of the maintenance pointlessly expended lower down. Not only was that stretch of road badly eroded, but at one point a small landslide had partly collapsed the side of a small hill across the road, and completely covered the drainage ditch. It looked almost like deliberate sabotage, an impression that was reinforced by the sight that greeted Zheng around the next corner. Here the landslide had wiped out half the road, and churned earth and an occasional bronze arrowhead in the mud showed that there had been recent fighting.

A military skirmish, or road bandits at work? Sometimes Zheng is glad he cannot read very well, or he would be tempted to peek at the dispatches he carries to discover what is happening around him. As it was, one thing was certain – Zheng should get away from there as soon as possible, and for the first time that day he kicked his horse into a full gallop.

Now, down from the pass, all is quiet, and though Zheng cannot get the memory of those arrowheads out of his mind, only a pheasant flapping its wings in the dense bush disturbs the peace of his solitary journey. A short plum tree stands on one side of the road, water droplets from a noon-time shower dripping from the round, pearl-shaped fruit, so Zheng uses his height on horseback to pluck a plum and bite into the sweet, juicy contents. He feels some of the tension from the crossing of the pass drain away, though he is still determined to report on what he has seen when he reaches the capital.

'If things are going smoothly, something is about to go wrong.' Zheng remembers this saying of his uncle's as he moves further downhill and sees that a few hundred metres away the road is completely blocked by a stationary cart. His superstitious and pessimistic uncle is one of the reasons that Zheng was so eager to get back to work. Even though the manager of the post station had assured him that other stations had picked up his load (and shared it with passing soldiers, who were pressed into carrying messages should they be going that way), Zheng really did not need yet another day of being told that his injury would have been avoided had he only refrained from travelling on an unlucky *xin ren* day.

To Zheng's grumpy response that he couldn't choose when and where he was sent, the uncle had remonstrated that Zheng should at least have consulted the star charts to see where the protector star *Taisui* was located in the sky before his departure. That way he would have known to avoid certain directions when traversing the countryside on his ill-fated journey. Now it occurs to Zheng that he had actually muttered a charm for protection and good luck as he had mounted his horse that morning. Prolonged exposure to his uncle's superstitions is clearly getting to him, although the cart blocking his way suggests that the charm might not have been particularly effective.

Zheng dismounts and greets the driver and his companion, who are so busy examining their vehicle that they do not hear him approach. 'Are you going to the capital?' asks the driver. 'How far is it?' His accent is unfamiliar.

There is a road running up the south-east flank of the hill, and Zheng assumes that the cart came along this route. A quick peek within the cart shows nothing but baskets covered with bamboo lids, so Zheng gives way to curiosity and asks what the carters are carrying.

In response, one man lifts the lid of one of the baskets to reveal a mass of loquat, with jagged leaves still attached to the stems of some of the fruit. Other baskets are filled with cherries. The driver anxiously informs him that the entire load must be at the capital before dusk, as the fruit is to be used for a ceremonial event. In fact the cart is running very late, because rough roads earlier had rolled the baskets about and some fruit became bruised. The pair had stopped at a local postal station to re-arrange their cargo, then tried to make up time by taking this shorter road and had become stuck.

'Two days' travel and now this afternoon is getting late!' remarks one of the men almost in despair. 'I don't think much of your post stations either. The one we stopped at overnight was run-down and looked abandoned. There was nothing to eat and since yesterday we have had nothing but water.'

And cherries, thinks Zheng cynically as he helps to drag the cart aside sufficiently for him to pull his horse through the gap. Before he leaves, he points out the direction to the city, where one of the highest towers is visible against the sky. 'It's closer than you imagine,' he tells the carters. 'Don't give up now.'

He climbs back upon his horse and gallops away. Over the next few minutes, he tells himself that indeed the outline of the tower of the Zhangcheng (eastern) gate is getting nearer. He seems almost able to pick out the individual tiles on the roof. Today, for sure, he will be able to deliver his message to the department of the interior well before sunset.

But he still remains anxious. Although he has just assured the carters that the city is not too far away, he knows that things seen in the distance can be deceptive. One always optimistically perceives one's destination as closer than it is in reality. Even now, although he has cleared the mountain pass, before he gets to the city there are still a few villages containing who knows what obstacles. The capital, its people, its walls and its buildings always, always, seem so distant and unreachable.

The Farmer
Takes a Break

The times change, and Xu has been quick to change with the times. This constantly surprises friends and neighbours, who wonder at the old curmudgeon's remarkable flexibility. The very land that Xu is now ploughing is further proof of that.

The family's former farm in Anyang, Henan prefecture, had been doing well enough, but nevertheless Xu had uprooted his family and moved them to Neihuang county, to a site beside the Yellow River where the land was richer and more fertile. Admittedly, the land was more fertile because for years it had lain fallow. The government used it as a floodplain to absorb the seasonal rising of the river and protect communities downstream.

Xu had noticed that the government was becoming lax in their punishment of farmers who moved on to this once strictly forbidden territory. 'They need us to cultivate the land,' he had argued to his father. 'Look at the size of the village, compared to when I was a boy. There are more houses, more people, and it's happening everywhere. The government needs us to feed all these extra people, and to feed the people we need land. Land is our lifeline, and there's rich fields waiting for us by the river. Let's not waste the opportunity!'

Bold and forward-looking Xu considered himself to be – reckless and opportunistic, others had argued – yet even so, Xu's family had almost arrived too late. Other even more enterprising folk had also moved into the fertile valley, and the only land still available on the floodplain had been on the furthest point from the newly built village.

Every day Xu complains to friends, family and neighbours about the distance he has to walk to his new fields, but secretly he is pleased and proud at how well his gamble has paid off. The land is indeed fecund, and crop yields are almost double those they used to harvest in Anyang. Each year, Xu and his family plant wheat in the winter and after the first harvest, they immediately sow the seeds of a summer crop. Last year's crop was soybeans and the substantial yield had been so immensely satisfying that this year Xu is going with the same again.

If this is another good year, Xu plans to get himself a pair of cattle. For today's work he has been forced to rent plough animals, and the results have been far from satisfactory. Xu grumbles to himself as he sees the furrow forming beneath the ploughshare. It's too shallow! No wonder when the mismatched team of a cow and a horse were all that he could scrounge from the neighbours. Animals are scarce because everyone else is ploughing too, and to make things worse the family insist on Xu keeping to the traditional restrictions on planting. Wheat should not be planted on the *xu* day and soybeans should not be planted on the *shenmao* day, just as his mother used to warn them.

'And decent plough animals can't be rented to suit our stupid family taboos,' fumes Xu to himself. 'I would have been able to use two cattle if I could have got them yesterday, but no,

A TILE RUBBING OF AN EASTERN HAN STONE
RELIEF DEPICTING A FARMER PLOUGHING. THE
IRON PLOUGHSHARE WAS A VITAL INVENTION
FROM THE HAN PERIOD

yesterday was *shenmao*. So now I have to do two hectares this afternoon with this pair – and they were already exhausted when I got them.'

Xu considers whipping the animals to make them go faster, but he doesn't because at heart he is a kindly man. He also knows that he would partly be acting out of the guilt he feels because his tight schedule means that his wife and daughter will have to come out to the field to help him for the rest of the afternoon. As if his wife did not have enough to do at home, tending to their infant son, shopping at the market, and tending to their newly acquired pigs, which have inexplicably gone off their feed.

Longingly, Xu thinks of the heavy steel ploughshare he has seen for sale in the village. Such things are becoming more common, and the local farmers gossip about how the new ploughshares are transforming farming. Not only do these ploughs break up heavy alluvial clays, but they do so quickly and leave a lovely deep furrow. Forget soybeans – with such a plough Xu could break up some of the currently unused land by the river bank and, who knows, maybe even plant summer cereals!

Xu would have got the ploughshare long ago except that such a plough needs to be pulled by a matched pair of cattle, and he can't afford that yet. Instead, he is plodding along behind the tails of a cow and a horse, as though he were some starving peasant of his grandfather's day, back when horses were hard to find, cattle even more so, and you had to plough with whatever you could get.

As they reach the end of a furrow, Xu wipes the sweat from his face and decides that as they have got through a large portion of the afternoon's work it is time to give his team a well-deserved rest. Settling himself against a clay embankment, he stares thoughtfully at the uncultivated land near the river bank. Flooding might be a problem there – in fact a severe flood of the Yellow River will threaten all his lands and those of his neighbours also.

There's constant talk of building new dams and dykes to hold back the waters, but Xu cynically reckons that while this is an excellent idea, it will not happen any time soon. Such a major project will need a huge investment of community resources (no one is naïve enough to expect any help from the local authorities), and a substantial number of villagers complacently believe that since the present hastily constructed levees along the riverbank have held back the waters so far, they can be expected to keep doing so.

So the murky river water continues to lap along its present banks, sending ripples along the channels. Mayflies are gathering above the reeds, their short lives due to end that evening. Xu gazes at the river, dreaming of going fishing soon on his boat. Whenever he has a free moment he likes to join his fellow villagers in fishing, hunting, or collecting wild berries and edible plants from the riverine environment.

These excursions do provide extra food for the village, and, dried and salted, the foodstuffs gathered make an essential reserve to get them through the inevitable lean years. Yet there is another reason why Xu joins these excursions. They are also opportunities for Xu to solidify and expand his social network and learn more about conditions in the wider community up and down the river.

Now Xu leads his mismatched team to the riverbank and ties the hemp rope to a nearby shrub, making sure there is plenty of fresh grass within range of the rope. Should either animal defecate while resting, Xu will add the manure to his fields, as he already does with the faeces of the pigs back at home. He tuts to himself, hoping his wife has persuaded the pigs to eat. They want the porkers fat and meaty when his son's first birthday ceremonies are due, but the pigs, like so much else these days, are an experiment for the family, and they are learning pig-rearing as they go along.

Also new is this idea of year-round farming. The innovative *Daitianfa* technique divides the field into ridges and furrows, so that seedlings grown in the furrows are protected from the wind and get plenty of water. Alternating the ridges and furrows each year extracts even more crops from the soil, and allows an extra annual harvest. Naturally, the government has been working hard to encourage farmers to adopt the new technique – even to the extent of sending agronomists such as the famous Zhao Guo out into the countryside to show farmers what to do.

If only the government had the farmers' interests in mind when they come up with these innovations, Xu often complains to friends. Instead, the result of agricultural breakthroughs has been to trap small farmers into an ever-deepening spiral of exploitation. The more crops they produce, the more the government takes in tax and, in the end, after a year of back-breaking labour, they are left with as much as they would have had in the old days after a single harvest.

Irritably, Xu picks up a harrow and starts breaking up clods of clay on the ridges. He does this with rather unnecessary force, and feels himself tiring fast. He has worked and sweated enough already today, so it is something of a relief to see his family approach, picking their way carefully across the new-ploughed furrows. His wife has their infant son balanced on her hip and carries a hoe on her shoulder, a basket dangling from one end and from the other a jar secured by a cord at the neck. His daughter carries another jar, and the family settle down to a picnic meal in the lengthening shadow of the trees that mark the boundary of their fields.

The daughter offers her father porridge and vegetables while her mother takes salted fish and bread from her basket. As she works, Xu's wife remarks on an odd sight that she spotted in the village. In the main square where some of the locals dry their crops, a government official was sitting on a blanket. He looked rather ridiculous, she giggles, sipping his refined tea while his elegant clothes were slowly covered in chaff.

Xu finds nothing ridiculous about this. The only government officials who ever visit regularly are taxmen, and they collected their dues only recently. Another explanation immediately comes to his suspicious mind – the man is a land assessor. The farmers on the floodplain have finally become prosperous enough to attract the attention of the local authorities, and now it seems that they have sent someone to determine who is farming what land, and exactly how much land each farmer claims.

To say that land assessors are unpopular is a wild understatement, as shown by the fact that outraged peasants have on occasion rioted after receiving their assessments. A corrupt assessor will vastly over-state the size of a farmer's holding, all the better to extract more tax from him, and even a scrupulous assessor will stretch to the maximum every inch of land he measures. Perhaps to calm popular unrest, the local authorities recently executed an over-zealous assessor whose measurements bore little resemblance to reality.

Xu looks across his fields to where his daughter is playing on the section still to be ploughed. However, what he actually sees is another thirtieth of his harvest vanishing into the insatiable maw of the government. This additional imposition might be bearable if other taxes were reduced, or even stayed the same, but Xu is not so naïve as to believe for a moment that this will happen. 'We take all the risks,' he fumes to himself. 'I and the other farmers work to build the dams, add infrastructure through our own labour, and risk starvation if the river floods or the crops fail. Yet when we achieve freedom or prosperity – it is taken away. What future awaits our children?'

A warning cry from his wife alerts him that his daughter is playing with the tail of the cow, and the animal is starting to get annoyed. This reminds Xu that he has much to do before it grows dark. They'll get the ploughing done today, but will sow the soybeans tomorrow, he decides. Stretching wearily, he goes to hitch the two animals to the plough once more while his wife chases their giggling daughter down along the levee.

The village buried under the Yellow River

The Sanyangzhuang site is situated on an abandoned Yellow River floodplain in Neihuang County, Henan Province. It was occupied by several farming compounds before *c.* AD 14 when the Yellow River breached the channel and covered the area with floodwater for several years.

Recent excavations of the site have revealed what a late Western Han farming village looked like. The exposed housing compounds had tiled roofs, food-processing facilities and possibly a loom, and probably a grove of mulberry trees.

THE CONVICT
ARRIVES AT HIS
DESTINATION

Now that the prisoners have stopped marching for the day, Tao's iron chains seem to have become even heavier, and the blisters and sores on his feet stab him with pain every time the line of prisoners shuffles slowly forward. Soon Tao is standing before an immaculately dressed government functionary. 'State your name, age, height, criminal charge, sentence, home county and prison name,' the functionary says, without even looking up at the man standing before him.

'Tao Sheng, twenty-four, seven feet [Han 'feet' are equal to about 23 cm], causing grievous bodily harm, sentenced to five years' hard labour, Pingyu County, and the county's detention house,' Tao replies in an emotionless voice. The registrar writes down the information quickly and finally looks up, taking a long look at Tao's iron chains and clothing. But he says nothing and Tao steps aside for him to register the next person.

Not only Tao, but thousands of convict labourers are on the move, some voluntarily, but most having been forcibly marched away from their homes and families. Conditions on these marches are brutal, and thousands of tragedies take place on the roads every day. Lives and memories pass away, fading unnoticed, just as the footprints of the prisoners quickly disappear from the dusty roads they are forced to travel.

For the past seven days, Tao has been in one of those long columns of shackled, suffering humanity, linked to the other prisoners not just by his chains but also through a shared sense of grievance. Tao is not the only prisoner who suspects that his sentence had less to do with the facts of his case and more to do with the empire's need for a large, mobile force of slave labourers.

Like many others on the lower levels of the social scale, Tao never had any expectation that the system would treat him fairly. He was born to poor parents who were tenant farmers for their entire lives. Like most such farmers, Tao's parents were desperately poor, and what little they put together was spent immediately on food to feed Tao and his starving siblings. Tao was the youngest child, and he lived with his elderly parents until first his father, and then his mother, passed away.

The death of his parents would have changed Tao's life anyway, but after his mother's death that change happened in the worst possible way. Because the family's grinding poverty had become even worse with the death of his father, the mother's funeral was a mean, cheap affair, and even that was more than Tao and his siblings could afford. Consequently, when some village rowdies began jeering at the evident poverty shown in the funeral arrangements, Tao had lost his temper and waded into the mockers with his fists. Hard work since early childhood had made Tao remarkably tough, and this, combined with his present fury, meant that he hit one man so hard that he fractured his skull.

The local authorities had no problems ignoring poverty, or even starvation in the village, but any breakdowns in law and order were dealt with quickly and severely. Tao was immediately taken to the detention cell inside the County Office and confined there for about a month until a judge could decide upon his guilt and sentence. Poor living conditions were nothing unusual for Tao, whose run-down thatched house was a standing joke among the villagers, but compared to the horrendously derelict condition of the detention cells, Tao's hovel had been a veritable paradise.

Ten other people shared Tao's tiny cramped cell, leaving not only little room to move about in the day but almost no floor space to sleep on at night. To show their indifference to the prisoners' suffering, the authorities not only made no attempt to improve conditions but even added two more prisoners to make Tao's last days of confinement even worse.

Why it took a month for his case to come to trial was a mystery to Tao, for after all, no one was disputing the facts of what should have been an open-and-shut case. It did occur to him that the government official who would adjudicate the matter was waiting deliberately in the hope that Tao's brothers – his only remaining family – needed time to gather the money needed to bribe the official into handing down a light sentence. If so, the man would be disappointed, for the family had spent their last coins on their mother's funeral. On the other hand, whatever sentence Tao received would not be influenced by the victim's family either – almost everyone in Tao's village was too poor to be able to offer a meaningful bribe.

Perhaps the official was disgruntled by the lack of financial return on his arbitration, or perhaps he had a quota of prisoners to feed into the government's labour supply; for whatever reason, the sentences he handed down that day were shockingly harsh. Tao was sentenced to five years' imprisonment with hard labour, to be served with his head shaved and his legs chained.

Tao's sentence was of the type known as *chengdan chong* – the most severe type of sentence male or female prisoners can receive short of the death penalty. *Chengdan* means 'building cities', while *chong* refers to dehusking rice. Initially, *chengdan chong* was a literal life sentence, but more recently this had been shortened to six, five or four years of labour service. The head-shaving ordered for Tao was a mild additional punishment, as some alternatives allow the authorities to cut off toes, make prisoners wear facial tattoos, or whipping.

The same day, two minor offenders who had been in the detention cells with Tao were given *guixin* (also called *guixin baican*) sentences of three years apiece. These prisoners would spend their sentences in temples doing tasks such as cutting timber. A female prisoner was given *baican*, which is the equivalent but with tasks better suited to female prisoners, such as picking rice and other types of menial labour.

These prisoners reacted to the injustice of their sentences with cries of utter anguish and outrage, beating their chests and stamping their feet as they wailed. Tao, on the other hand, remained stoically calm, telling himself that there was nothing to cry about. With the death of his parents, their land had been given to other tenants to farm, so even if he were a free man, he would be landless, homeless and jobless. At least as a prisoner he would get shelter and meals of some description.

Nevertheless, it was worrying to see the jailer weeping quietly when the news came that Tao and the others would be working on an imperial project in Chang'an. The jailer was a kindly old man who had done his best for the prisoners under

Convict labourers

The five main types of sentence were *chengdan chong, guixin, lichen, sikou* and *fazuo*, based on how many years convict labourers would serve in jail.

Compared to the first two categories, *lichen* convicts enjoyed much more freedom. Male convicts were called *lichen* while female convicts were called *liqie*. Essentially, they were required to serve in the governmental offices performing a wide range of menial, often dreary tasks. Some *lichen* even delivered governmental documents, which meant that they could move around freely. After the reform of criminal laws during the middle Western Han, *lichen* was not used for convict labourers any more.

Sikou was originally a title for governmental officers. It became a sentence during the Qin-Han period and referred to one of the lightest punishment options during this time. *Sikou* convicts could even participate in managerial work in the prisons. For instance, some Qin-period law documents have been discovered on bamboo slips that state that *sikou* oversaw the labour work of the *chengdan chong* convict labourers. Every twenty *chengdan chong* were watched over by one *sikou*. Some *sikou* could even possess their own land, although their right of land ownership was only equal to half that of commoners'.

Fazuo also refers to a light sentence and some scholars think that it was the same as *fuzuo*, a sentence used with female convicts. A *fazuo* sentence normally involved one year or several months of light labour, perhaps the equivalent of modern community service.

his care. He had cleaned the cell as best he could and made sure everyone had enough water to drink. He could do little about the poor quality of the food, but he had at least passed on to Tao the food that his older brothers had sent to him. Many another jailer would have 'confiscated' the food and sold it for private profit. Even with the help of his brothers, though, Tao was still malnourished, and like the other prisoners, he was sickly and weak even before his debilitating march.

The old jailer had shared in the general excitement when a rumour swept through the cells that the emperor was planning a general pardon across the country for many criminals. Even those who remained would have their iron shackles removed, and they would not have to do their work in demeaning convict's clothing. In fact the jailer had seemed more excited than Tao, who had just shrugged with apparent indifference to whatever fate awaited him.

In any case, it turned out that the rumours were wrong, although the imperial bureaucrats did indeed have plans for their convict labourers. They were to be sent to build canals, imperial mausoleums and other imperial infrastructure projects. Tao and his fellow convicts were part of a group designated to build ceremonial temples in Chang'an, a project that the new emperor, Wang Mang, was personally interested in and anxious to complete.

After the announcement was made public, Tao discovered the reason for the jailer's distress. During his long career, the old man had seen many prisoners marched off to labour on construction projects, and he knew how few of them would ever come back, and how those who did return would do so broken in body and spirit.

On the day when the convict labourers were scheduled to depart, their families and relatives came to bid them farewell, and exchange what many rightly feared would be their last words with their loved ones. So crowded was the courtyard outside the county prison that Tao and his brothers were squeezed into a corner, with Tao's back almost impaled against the hedge of thorn bushes planted around the prison to prevent escape. The sharp spines digging into his back and the screech of irritated birds within the hedge had made Tao hot and dizzy. He became very impatient when one of his brothers started to tell him to look after himself and not take any unnecessary risks. How was he supposed to do that? The brothers had not parted on the best of terms, but Tao tells himself this does not matter. He will probably never see them again anyway.

The convicts were marched west for almost seven days. At night, they were left to sleep in the open, without blankets or any kind of shelter. The food consisted of a few meals of decayed cereal grudgingly handed out at the end of each day's journey. With each passing mile the convict labourers became more exhausted and their uniforms increasingly filthy and tattered. Tao grew ever more taciturn and withdrawn, and seldom joined in his companions' lamentations about their wretched situation.

It is not so long since the Qin dynasty was overthrown, in part because of the imperial fondness for forcing the population into unpaid labour on government projects. Yet, after just a relatively short period of the 'governance by doing nothing' policy, the convicts bitterly observe, the Han government has started to adopt the ways of their Qin predecessors, and now the bad old days are back. Hundreds of thousands of forced labourers slave away at government projects both practical and impractical, and where the work is especially difficult or dangerous, convict labour is found – even if the crimes of the prisoners don't even come close to matching the punishment.

So today has been their last day on the road, and after giving his details to the registrar, Tao has time to look around at his destination. He had not really paid much attention while they were on the march, even when a few hours ago they had approached a large quarry that many of the convicts had assumed marked the end of their journey. So brutal had been the march that the convicts even envied the line of quarry workers shifting cartloads of yellow earth.

As it is, the convicts have halted beside what appears to be a large, poorly maintained graveyard. There are no trees, no houses, not even any birds hovering above in the sky, just the large cemetery on their right. Tao begins to suspect that this is the place where dead convict labourers are buried, and judging from the confused commotion coming from the column, other prisoners are coming to the same conclusion.

The overseers are reluctant to answer shouted questions about the graveyard, but to quiet the prisoners they explain to them that they are one *li* away from their base, and the construction site for the temples is one *li* beyond that. They have only stopped here to register all the convicts in the column before they spend the night with the general population of workers already on the site.

With the prisoners registered, the column begins to move slowly along once more. Tao watches a soldier whipping a group of labourers as they carry loads to an unknown destination, and so is surprised when they abruptly halt at a mat-walled shelter beside a small earthen mound.

He hears an overseer shouting, 'Find your own cell where you will be sleeping tonight. You start working tomorrow!' Tao's group duck through the doorway, though this is hardly necessary – they could almost as easily have entered through gaps in the walls that are only slightly larger than the many holes in the roof.

Some of Tao's fellow convict labourers, who just moments ago were looking forward to finally completing their march, start to weep upon seeing their final destination. This is the place where they are going to spend the night and hundreds of nights to come. Tao is disappointed with what he has seen, but he silently agrees with the more optimistic convicts that at least tonight they will sleep under a roof, even a pathetic excuse for a roof such as this is. As usual, Tao does not join in the general discussion, and though his silence clearly irritates some of his fellow convicts, his reputation for violence keeps them from expressing their criticism aloud.

Soon there is another wave of uproar and a bitter litany of obscene complaints from the convict labourers. They have discovered that their monthly food ration is to be less than three *dan* per person – a tiny amount not even sufficient to feed a small pig. It is considerably less than the soldiers' rations, and the soldiers will be mostly standing around watching the convicts doing the heavy work.

One of two convicts who have got to know Tao while they were on the move now looks at him and asks in a low voice, 'Are we going to put up with this, then?' Once, Tao might have bitterly pointed out that there was no other choice, but in the past few days these two convicts have been quietly pointing out that there is indeed one other option – open rebellion.

When there were no overseers and soldiers present to overhear, these two prisoners had reminded Tao of convict mutinies in Yingchuan, Shanyang and other places. There, the insurrectionists had captured and burned down governmental offices, killed officers and freed prisoners. In his turn, Tao had reminded the would-be rebels that all these insurrections had ended in failure. None of the prisoners had escaped – in fact most of them had not even managed to get away with their lives, for the government had invariably reacted with extreme force.

Yet it is now clear that the prisoners will be treated worse than dogs. Tao's fate is to be worked to death and then buried in that large graveyard beside which he had been registered as a labourer. Under such circumstances, he has absolutely nothing to lose, and this pushes him to a decision.

Tao had been told that as the prisoners settle into their cells for the evening, soldiers will come to check the chains on their feet. They will put heavy iron collars on the prisoners to keep them chained together, but the wrist shackles will be removed so that the convicts can do their work more easily on the morrow. There will be a moment when their hands are free but their necks have not yet been shackled, and this might present an opportunity – if not, there will be others.

Tao makes an agreed-upon gesture to the two convict labourers, signalling that he has become fully committed to their plans, and that they urgently need to discuss things right now.

酉 TWELFTH HOUR OF THE DAY

(17.00–18.00: FIRST PART OF *YOU*)

THE KILN WORKER FEELS HOUNDED

After days like this Su feels that he should never have left the pottery business. At the time, the move from making pottery to baking bricks had seemed like a good idea. Su had been a craftsman in a private workshop that specialized in making high-stemmed *dou* plates. Su was good at that job, and fully intended to spend the rest of his working life doing it. Unfortunately, the region has a lot of skilled craftsmen making high-stemmed *dou* plates, and competition in the market grew so fierce that, like many older businesses, Su's workshop proved unable to compete with the new factories that seemed to be opening up everywhere.

When the workshop closed its doors, Su shifted to a large organization that produced only a single product: large cheap jars. Though cheap, these jars were hardly good value for money as they were not watertight and crumbled almost at a touch. It offended Su's sense of professional ethics that he should be making a product that he would not want to buy for himself, so he left the job after only a year.

This may have seemed reckless for a man with a wife and son to support, but Su knew that men with experience with fired clay were much in demand – not so much in the overcrowded pottery business, but in making and baking bricks. Across the country, a building boom is under way. New public buildings are being erected at an unprecedented rate, and wealthy families are busily constructing manor houses for themselves to live in and large brick tombs where they plan to remain after death.

While buildings of the previous Qin dynasty attempted to appeal through the sheer magnificence of their bulk, Han buildings – while no less substantial – are also spectacularly beautiful. Yet from the roofs that so carefully evoke different shapes, such as flying birds and mountain ridges, all the way down to the elegantly creative patterns on the floors, the sweat of kiln workers is embedded into every brick.

The rural landscape of Han China is dotted with the chimneys of brick-and-tile manufactories where workers struggle to keep up with incessant demand for their product. Since this is one field where his skills will never become redundant, it seemed an obvious step for Su to transfer his craft from the pottery to the brick-making industry. As he

A CLAY BRICK ENGRAVED WITH A PHOENIX BEFORE A TREE OF LIFE
(206 BC–AD 9)

had hoped, Su was almost at once eagerly recruited by a small government-run brick-and-tile factory, which was working at full capacity to meet its quota of the government's insatiable need for building materials to fuel its infrastructure projects.

The pay and the hours were good, and Su had reckoned that he would be able to handle the hard physical work at the kiln, but recently he had been forced to admit that he had underestimated the intensity of the work involved. The hard physical labour has also taken its toll on Su's fellow workers, and both his assistants sent notes that morning to inform him that they were unwell.

With no option, Su had been forced to recruit his son as a temporary worker, as it was simply impossible for him to do his first task of the morning alone. That job involved getting the day's delivery of clay loaded into a small cart and transported to a straw mat in the middle of the factory, where it would be left for processing. Even with Su pushing one end of the cart and his son pulling on the other, it was back-breaking work, for the son was unpractised at such labour, and was still only a boy. At around this point Su's usual good humour began fading fast.

At noon, his son had to get home, leaving Su alone in the factory. He did as much as he could, but really, brick-making is not a one-man operation. He refilled the water tank in the corner of the shed, and then took a quick lunch while he waited to see if any of his assistants were planning to turn up for the afternoon. He spent the first two hours after lunch mixing the clay that he and his son had earlier brought into the shed, and then pressing the wooden mould to make the thin square bricks required for floors.

It was a slow business shifting between all these tasks by himself, and when Su finally decided to quit brick-making he observed with mild disgust that he had only managed to make two small rows of floor bricks, which he had left to dry on the western side of the shed. It appears that today he is not going to be able to keep up with the normal routine, in which, as a batch of bricks is being fired in the kilns, another batch is being prepared and set aside to dry under the shed. Finally, deciding that he was going to have to fire the kilns by himself, Su set about preparing the fuel.

The kilns use a mixture of firewood and cereal chaff, and getting a kiln stacked with a full load of fuel involves multiple trips with their small cart. Usually Su would leave this job to one of his co-workers, not because the task is particularly onerous, but because for some reason he reacts very badly to the bits of cereal chaff that always end up floating about in the air while the cart is being loaded. Today, though, he has no choice but to do it himself and after just three cartloads he is doubled over and coughing so violently that he decides to stop or he will be unable to do anything else for the rest of the day. It occurs to him that he might perhaps pour a little water over the chaff, and he makes a note to give this a try later.

For now, he has transported sufficient fuel for two kilns, and that – along with the fuel that was stacked there yesterday when the workshop had its full complement of staff – will have to be enough to be going on with. Su looks about, mentally prioritizing the jobs that remain to be done.

The spacious shed that serves as their workshop is divided into areas, each dedicated to a particular aspect of their craft. The large space between the two foundation stones faces west, and as that catches the sun for most of the day, the area is reserved for air-drying bricks. Half of the shed space is currently taken up by several rows of unfired wall bricks that they made three days ago. The eastern part of the shed is set at a slightly lower level, all the better to allow water from the clay-preparation process and brick-making to properly drain into the water tank outside.

The factory has sets of wooden moulds for brick-making that allows the workers to prepare different types of brick according to the needs of their customers. For the past few months they have been making large quantities of the small-sized bricks about 20–30 cm long, 10–15 cm wide and 5 cm thick that are typical of the Han period, and a marked contrast to the super-sized bricks used in buildings of the Qin era.

They were warned by their manager that these bricks are required for the court of the county governor, and if the building is to match the prestige of the office, the brickwork has to be of a matching quality. So the clay is not to be adulterated with the usual materials that help to stretch their stocks further, and the thick, elongated bricks that will become the walls are of the same high standard as the thinner square bricks that will eventually become the governor's tiled floor. The plan calls for the roofs of different parts of the building to rise one above the other, with the baked tiles of the eaves forming a variety of harmoniously blended patterns. It's an ambitious plan, and so far Su's workshop has been one of the main sources of the bricks that are making the architect's vision a reality.

Su has been working at a fairly relaxed pace, for after all no one can reasonably expect him to manage a full day's production by himself. What is to be done about his absent helpers is fortunately not his decision, as their absence will be on the record – along with other absences that have been getting more numerous of late, and eventually the manager will have to do something about it.

Thinking about the manager's reaction to the day's severely reduced production causes Su to realize that the afternoon is almost done and he has not yet loaded any of the air-dried bricks into the kilns for firing. There are two groups of kilns at one end of the work-shed, with six kilns in each group. Usually Su and his helpers each look after two of the kilns in each group, but today Su needs to load bricks in all six kilns by himself. The manager will probably be over to check the quality of the bricks tomorrow afternoon and if Su wants to have something to show him, the air-dried wall bricks need to be loaded into the kilns for firing overnight so that they can be taken out tomorrow morning to cool.

Su returns once again to the cart – which is by far the hardest-working device in the shed – and takes it to the brick pile, selecting those that are completely dry and ready to be fired. Once he has found a suitable batch, the cart is quickly loaded and Su sets off for the kiln, casting a quick glance back at all the unfired bricks under the shed. Barely half of the first row of the bricks fitted into his cart. He is going to have to go back and forth with cartload after cartload under the hot afternoon sun before he has even begun to make significant progress – and it does not help that the kilns in the group he is not using are still radiating heat from yesterday's operations. It is because the baked clay of the kilns holds the heat for so long after the fires have been extinguished that there are two groups of kilns, so that one set of six can cool down while the other group is in use.

Su takes off his singlet and uses it to wipe his face, but sweat continues to drip from head to toe. His face is smeared with clay made into streaks by his sweat, and his trousers are completely soaked. Su wants to stop, take a long, cool drink and rehydrate in the shade, but time is short and he is getting more worried about his progress, or lack of it.

Coming back from stacking yet another load, Su comes upon an unexpected sight. One of his co-workers, Ding, has decided to show up and is now sitting in a corner unhurriedly heating up a small *zun* jar containing wine. As Su comes storming over, Ding removes the wine from the heat – heaven knows why he wants to heat his wine in a workshop that feels to Su like a blast furnace – and takes a leisurely sip.

In his exasperation, Su forgets to feel grateful at finally having an extra set of hands to help out. 'What are you doing, Ding?' he demands. 'Why do you think you have time to enjoy your wine now? Look around, is it not busy enough for you?' Su is so annoyed that he forgets to ask why Ding did not show up for work that day, as the man is obviously not sick.

Ding answers casually, 'What is the rush? I need to drink my wine and warm up before doing any heavy work.'

'What is the rush?' Su repeats Ding's question. 'I have been running non-stop like a rat since this morning. Open your eyes; can't you see that the day is almost done and we still have so much to do!' Su is so infuriated he is almost ready to throw a brick at Ding.

It is aggravating that Su can't really order Ding to do anything – that's the manager's prerogative, and what is more infuriating still is that the manager will assume that Su and Ding shared today's workload between them. Consequently, Su is in no good temper as he picks up the last few bricks from the first row to put them in the cart.

He notices something and pauses, spotting that the bricks have a not-unattractive pattern of paw prints wandering across them. He shakes his head in disapproval, making a note to remind his co-workers yet again that they really have to secure the doors of the shed if they are the last to leave in the evening. Given that there is no substantial black market for sun-dried unfired brick, and that the bricks in the kiln are too hot to handle, the shed does not need to be locked to prevent items being taken out. Rather, the problem is that something might get in – a drunk looking for somewhere to urinate, or a dog that considers a pile of drying bricks to be a sort of canine adventure playground.

If the bricks were for a private construction project, then the paw prints might yet be acceptable to the builders if they were offered a small discount. That is not going to happen for the current project, where only the best will do. Su can imagine what the manager would say about paw prints when he carefully scrutinizes the bricks during tomorrow's inspection. Irritably, Su takes these last few bricks from the cart and throws them on the floor so that he can recycle them later.

Another kiln is almost ready to be loaded, so Su unpacks the last few bricks and holds them to his chest as he carefully walks down to the subterranean pit connected to the kiln. He stoops to get through the short door and (being careful not to stir the accursed chaff up into his lungs again) steps onto the soft cereal chaff that he had put in the fire chamber earlier that morning. He stretches his arms to reach the main chamber of the kiln and carefully lays down the bricks he has been carrying. Backing out of the kiln, he repeats the procedure three times until he has unloaded the entire cart of bricks, after which he makes a quick calculation that he needs two more stacks of bricks to fill up the chamber.

Meanwhile, Ding has finished his wine and is loading bricks onto his cart from the far end of the shed. Deciding that he can take a small break now that Ding's arrival has effectively halved his workload, Su decides to finally treat himself to a long drink of water. As Ding goes past with his cartload of bricks, Su makes a suggestion – he will carry on taking the bricks to the kiln and loading them if Ding brings the firewood and corn chaff for the other kilns. That way Ding gets to avoid doing the heavy lifting, and Su's lungs are spared the hated chaff. Ding nods his head in agreement and pushes his cart to the far end of the factory. That half-jar of wine seems to have had no effect on his movements, but Su knows that Ding has a taste for very cheap wines, and the stuff he was drinking was probably closer to water in any case.

Su stacks up another two piles of bricks in the firing chamber of the kiln and turns his attention to the flues. There are three flues located at the rear wall of the main chamber, which gradually join halfway up the wall into one large funnel-shaped chimney at the top of the kiln. After ensuring that the flues are clear, Su walks to the back of the kiln to check that the chimney is not currently blocked. He also checks that there is a large brick nearby, as this will later be used to partly block the chimney once the oven starts heating up, thus ensuring that the temperature of the reducing flame inside the kiln remains high and consistent throughout the night.

All that is needed now is to start the fire, then put in the chimney brick once the fire has properly caught, and that will be another kiln done. Su notes with some dissatisfaction that he has around another two hours yet before he can leave the factory; he's under no illusions that Ding will offer to stay longer to make up for the hours he missed this morning. Su had told his son that he might be able to get home in time for dinner, but that looks less likely now. He wonders whether his son will come to the workshop and find him again, because with an extra pair of hands helping to finish the job, dinner together might yet be a possibility.

In a more optimistic mood, he goes to collect another cartload of bricks from the other half of the second row, and this is when he discovers where the dog had gone after it had left paw prints all over the first row of bricks. Quickly, Su turns from the ruined bricks and walks over to inspect the next row, praying all the while that the wandering hound had left these alone, for if yet another row has been spoiled, they won't have enough bricks to finish loading the kilns.

酉 FIRST HOUR OF THE NIGHT

(18.00–19.00: SECOND PART OF *YOU*)

THE CHEF PREPARES A BANQUET

He did not dislike to have his rice finely cleaned, nor to have his minced meat cut quite small. He did not eat rice which had been injured by heat or damp and turned sour, nor fish or flesh which was gone. He did not eat what was discoloured, or what was of a bad flavour, nor anything which was ill-cooked, or was not in season. He did not eat meat which was not cut properly, nor what was served without its proper sauce.

Xiangdang (In the Village) chapter, Analects of Confucius

Just as Ren walks into the kitchen, the scene of frantic preparation before him comes to a frozen halt at the sound of a heavy jar dropping to the floor and shattering into a hundred pieces. This is no uncommon occurrence, but, every time, the sound gets Ren's heart racing and his fists clenching. 'What happened?' Ren almost yells, and everyone turns to look at a junior helper who stands at a side table by the kitchen stove, his sandals splattered with the sauce that testifies to his clumsiness. The young man does not dare to look at Ren, but stands with his head held low, literally quivering with fear. Ren does not need to be told which pot was broken – naturally it was the one that contains his special fish sauce, the one that takes the most time to prepare.

After giving the culprit a long, thoughtful glare, Ren turns to the under-chef and mutely gestures to the shelf where he keeps his ingredients. After working with Ren for years, the under-chef understands at once that he should start preparing the ingredients for a new batch of sauce, which Ren will prepare as soon as he has the chance. That will not be immediately, for tonight – yet again – is a banquet night, and Ren has literally dozens of separate operations to oversee in his kitchen.

Ren has a highly prestigious job as head chef to the official heir of the Changsha princedom, and one of the requirements of the job is an ability to cope with extreme stress while doing half-a-dozen things at once. Since the Changsha princedom is one of the richest in the Han Empire, the heir, Liu, holds many banquets in the course of the year, and in keeping with the station of their host, the guests expect the most luxurious dishes and the most ostentatious entertainment. Late spring and early summer are particularly busy, for that is when the heir throws a multitude of banquets, sometimes as a representative of the king, and at other times on his own behalf. Important officials, royal relatives and rich landowners, powerful merchants and other trade groups, all need to see that they are valued and enjoy royal favour, and it is Ren's job to ensure that the food at the banquets is one sign of the prince's esteem.

Banquets put a lot of pressure on Ren, for the extra work involved in preparing for a banquet comes on top of his dozens of other duties, which include overseeing the sourcing and preparation of a large variety of cooking ingredients and the routine maintenance of the kitchen and its equipment.

Then there is the completely different set of skills required to successfully forge the two dozen individuals who work in the kitchen into a team that works well even through high-pressure events such as tonight.

In fact tonight will probably rank as one of the toughest evenings in a stressful year, for the heir will be entertaining his brother and his brother's retinue. As soon as he heard the news from the Steward of the Court, Ren (suppressing a groan of exasperation) knew he needed to get the best wine ready and prepare the most extravagant dishes in his repertoire. Everyone in the court of the heir knows about the intense and entirely pointless rivalry between him and his brother. It is not as if they have anything to fight over – Liu is the official heir, and this is as unalterable as if it were set in stone.

Within the bureaucratic system, the heir has convincingly demonstrated his diplomatic talent and leadership skills, and his ability as a future leader of the state is unquestioned. Yet despite this, the younger brother seems to take a perverse pleasure in the dangerous game of provoking and outdoing the designated heir. His reckless behaviour puts many people in a difficult position – not only members of his own retinue but also many of Liu's servants.

Ren certainly considers himself and his catering staff to be among the victims of this silly sibling rivalry. He is getting rather tired of Liu's foolish attempts at outdoing his younger brother – for what exactly does the heir need to prove? Those in the heir's retinue are also getting terribly frustrated with the constant need for new ideas to entertain this most difficult and picky of guests.

A typical official banquet should always emphasize order and hierarchy. The elderly guests should be shown due respect and the host should always preside over the banquet with appropriate manners. Yet as the prince's brother sometimes demonstrates, often-times at banquets manners are forgotten and hierarchy is not always honoured. For some, banquets are the place where they challenge and override the social order. Ren knows that everyone at the palace is desperately hoping that tonight's banquet will not be one such occasion.

Leaving his under-chef to deal with the hapless assistant and the broken sauce pot, Ren steps into the relatively calm and orderly atmosphere of where the wine-brewers work in their separate cellar that adjoins the main kitchen. As Ren enters, the head brewer is holding a jug filled with yellowish liquor mould made from fermented sticky rice, and this he is pouring into the long neck of a vat full of cooled, cooked rice that stands at one end of a long table. The head brewer stirs the liquor mould well and then carefully seals the vat with the lid attached to the neck.

The brewer then turns to the other side of the table, where another five vats stand in a row. Ren waits quietly as the brewer walks slowly along the row rapping each vat with his knuckles and nodding in apparent satisfaction at the resulting sound. When the brewer reaches Ren, the chef asks for a reminder of which flavours have been added to each vat. The head brewer lists the vats from left to right, proudly indicating each with a finger as he does so. The vats contain, respectively, rice wine, sticky millet (broomcorn millet) wine, sticky rice wine (plain) and two final vats where the wine is flavoured, one with honey and the other with fruit.

Ren ponders – which wine should he serve tonight? While he thinks it over, the head brewer goes to help one of his assistants,

who is filtering the rice wine from the vat on the left. The wine liquor is actually quite clear already, but the assistant is using their finest filter to make the wine as free of dregs as is humanly possible.

Others in the room are also working on filtering their own wines, so the musty smell pervades the entire room and mixes with the steam coming from a large pot of cooked rice in the corner. For the filtering, six large basins have been placed underneath the table next to several wine jars. Two brewers decant and transfer the fermented liquor from a vat to a basin, while one worker holds a mesh to filter out the dregs. When that operation is complete, the brewers will then pour the liquor into the wine jars while filtering it for a second time.

Ren watches the light yellowish liquor being decanted and comes to a decision. The rice wine went down very well last time, so well, in fact, that one guest, a rich merchant, managed to put away almost twenty cups of the stuff. Ren will offer that wine again tonight, and he accordingly writes three characters in red ink on a wine jar. The message is clear and not particularly subtle – the three characters, *shang zun jiu*, mean 'the best rice wine'. The red ink looks suitably festive, and the message is meant to assure the elite guests that their host is not stinting on quality.

Like many other royal palaces and aristocratic residences, the crown prince's palace stocks different wines for different banquets, ceremonies and other occasions, as well as keeping a reserve of small jugs to be given as gifts to the deserving. Although the brewers in Ren's kitchen work practically non-stop in shifts, they can only produce a small proportion of the wines needed by the prince's court. It never fails to amaze Ren how much wine he has to source and bring in to satiate the apparently bottomless thirst of the courtiers and their guests. While he is in the brewery, Ren designates wine for another approaching event by writing a line of characters on two other lacquered wine jars, one with elaborate decorative motifs on the surface, and the other with four birds standing on the lid.

That's the Han aristocracy, he thinks. They eat no rice but the finest quality, and they drink no wine except that produced from the finest cereals. Banquets are the perfect demonstration of their extravagant lifestyle. No matter how many rounds of wines are produced and how many delicious dishes are served, the next banquet must have finer wines, and food served on still more elegant platters.

Ren offers a last few words of appreciation to the brewers for their orderly operation. Then, just before heading back to the kitchen, he reminds them that, at the lead table where his Highness-to-be and the main guests will be seated, the steward should place jade cups with gold-ringed rims. No sooner has he left the brewery than he returns, having remembered the need to prompt the brewers to bring wine warmers when they take the wine to the hall.

In contrast to the measured, orderly operation of the wine brewery, the kitchen is now barely contained pandemonium as almost two dozen people work simultaneously on different aspects of the coming meal. The already cramped space is getting ever more congested and stuffy, and a junior chef tenderizing fish is doing little to improve conditions. The man is pouring with sweat as his well-muscled arms swing the mallet with which he has been beating the fish ever since Ren was last in the kitchen over half an hour ago. Judging by the state of the fish, the job is now almost finished.

Next to the junior chef two girls squat on the floor pulverizing herbs and nuts in a stone mortar, one pounding with a stone pestle while the other holds the mortar in place. Another group of teenage girls squats around two large shallow basins washing vegetables. Being girls with a mischievous side, they start to splash water at each other. An older woman supervising from her place near the stove tolerates this until the first vegetable is thrown, upon which, without turning around, she expertly hits the head of the offender with a backhand swing of her metal cooking ladle. The girl starts to cry, and as she gingerly rubs the spot where the ladle dinged her head, her loose chignon comes undone and her hair falls over her tear-stained face.

Ren has become numb to such dramas and petty scenes. It is his private opinion that the stress of trying to achieve ever more astonishing culinary creations for the prefecture court is driving everybody mad. Anyway, kitchens are too busy for formal disciplinary hearings when summary physical chastisement will do. He remembers that when he was young, he was regularly beaten by senior members of the kitchen, and he tells himself that this never held him back.

He steps around the wildly flying knife of a kitchen assistant frantically chopping vegetables, takes down a saucepan, and starts to prepare his sauce. Fish sauces are very popular in elite culinary culture and most chefs prepare their own signature sauces from carefully guarded recipes. Ren's recipe comes from his grandfather, who was not a professional chef, but a remarkably talented cook nonetheless. Ren's secret ingredients for his sauce include red-tail carp, orange rinds, fern leaves, some purple leaves and fish roe.

Depending on the type of fish being served, Ren will sometimes also add preserved bamboo shoots or mulberry tree leaves to enrich the flavour. This results in a light, slightly sour taste and a crunchy texture – a perfect combination that has won Ren's sauce the respect and admiration of the court.

As Ren is mixing and stirring the ingredients on the platform by the stove, a kitchen supervisor is instructing two helpers to prepare and cut vegetables on the platform once Ren has finished. Ren is not too worried about the preparation of vegetables, as he knows that this process rarely goes wrong with his trusted supervisor in charge. But he casts a quick glance over the washed greens in any case, seeing bamboo shoots, lotus roots and some salad leaves. Ren tells the supervisor to also prepare some small soybean leaves, as these will go well with his sauce tonight.

Through the tiny kitchen window Ren sees that the sky outside is starting to get dark and he suddenly feels the pressure all over again. Meat! Where is the meat? Is it prepared? Ren yells the questions aloud and is answered by another supervisor who shouts back across the hubbub of the kitchen.

'Yes, the swan meat is here. We've butchered three swans and are washing and preparing the meat now. The venison will be here in a minute.'

As if on cue, a voice hails the kitchen from outside. Two men have entered the yard carrying a large chopping board, upon which lies half of the deer that they have just butchered near the pen. The other half is on the way, one of the porters explains, but they brought this half so that the cooks can get started with cutting and marinating it. Ren eyes the blood dribbling off the edges of the board, and decides that there is no time to hang the carcass to drain. Yet he certainly does not want to get blood all over his kitchen floor, so he tells the men to leave the venison on the table outside.

The schedule is getting tight and there is still a great deal more to be done. Before they can grill the venison, they need to skin the carcass and marinate the meat. Ren hands a sharp knife to an under-chef and hustles the man outside to get started on the job. Then, once a quick check assures Ren that his kitchen is in a functional state of organized chaos, he decides to speed things up by helping the under-chef prepare the venison. With

Soup etiquette

Geng (soup) was an important food for the Han elites. In the *qiance* list (an inventory list of burial goods) in the Mawangdui tombs, five types of soup were recorded: *dageng* soups (plain meat without the five-spiced flavours); *baigeng* (meat broth with rice); *jingeng* (meat broth with celery); *fenggeng* (meat broth with green leaves); and *kufeng* (meat broth with 'the bitter vegetable' – common sow thistle).

These thick soups were consumed on important occasions for they had social implications and, therefore, had to be eaten according to certain rules of etiquette. One should never let the liquid dribble from one's mouth; and the meat in the soup should be eaten slowly and silently. In addition, a guest offered this soup should add neither salt nor any other seasoning, because to do so would suggest that the host had not prepared the soup to perfection.

the ease of long practice, the two effortlessly peel off the skin and start to chop the meat into large chunks. Ren will only feel at ease when he sees these cut hunks of venison being washed and marinated with salt and herbs by assistants back in the kitchen.

Ren is watching the gate, anticipating the arrival of the second half of the deer, but to his surprise, it is the Steward of the Court who steps through. 'Ren, what is the main meat course for tonight?'

'Venison from a two-year-old deer,' Ren replies, somewhat bewildered as to why the steward is asking this question now.

'Discard it! His Highness wants us to serve venison that is as tender as possible. Tell the butchers to slaughter a fawn!' From the tone in which the steward gives the order, Ren knows that it probably came direct from the prince, which leaves him no room for negotiation. It is clear that the steward understands how difficult a situation the royal whim has made things for the kitchen staff, for, after throwing Ren an embarrassed look, he hurries off, leaving a despairing Ren to work out how to find and prepare the meat for the changed menu.

They have only one fawn in the pens and that will certainly not be enough for twenty guests. Ren casts a speculative eye at the meat he has already cut, knowing that it is highly unlikely that any of the guests has so discerning a palate that they can tell the difference between the well-marinated flesh of a fawn and that of a young deer.

However, he discards the idea almost before it is formed, not from fear, although the punishment would be severe if it was discovered that the meat was not as had been stipulated. Rather, Ren believes that an order is an order and there is nothing for him to do but execute it to the best of his professional ability.

He takes a moment to assess the situation, and bounces back quickly from his momentary dismay. Reckoning the situation might be salvageable after all, he quickly summons two of his most capable assistants and instructs them to take over in the kitchen and make sure the vegetables and cereals are cooked properly. One assistant is put in charge of the boiled rice and steamed wheat-flour bread, and Ren takes the second assistant aside and points at the cut venison in the basins. He instructs the man to finish marinating the venison so that the kitchen has a backup plan – venison from an older deer is still better than no venison at all.

Ren intends to sprint to the butcher's shops outside the palace and requisition the first two fawns he sees. He steps back into the kitchen and wraps two sharp knives in cloth. Once he has found his booty, he intends to butcher and dress the meat on the spot – his royal master has left him with not a second to spare.

戌 SECOND HOUR OF THE NIGHT

(19.00–20.00: FIRST PART OF *XU*)

THE CONSORT'S MAID IS DISTRESSED

As they amble alongside the twin gate towers of the mausoleum, Wei and her maid enjoy the last few moments of the sunset, the last of the rosy golden-tinted hues filling the sky as the sun sinks below the horizon. It is strangely quiet. All the soldiers have gone home and the night guards have not yet reported for duty. Down the Spiritual Way, the central axis of the mausoleum, two rows of stone sculptures silently stand guard, their slender silhouettes, outlined against the sunlight, hinting at lost legends told in the language of long ago.

Wei remarks, 'You can never tell about life – one moment you are at the peak and everything is going smoothly and the next moment everything crashes, breaks apart and is lost forever, and then you reach your lowest point.' The maid nods thoughtfully in acknowledgement, even though she hears this particular pearl of wisdom at least once a day.

The maid has never known that 'peak' of which her mistress speaks, for she was assigned to Wei's service after her lady had

**ONE OF THE STONE SCULPTURES FOUND AT THE TOMB
OF THE HAN GENERAL HUO QUBING**

fallen from favour in the imperial court. But Wei talks about it often – sometimes the maid feels a bit disloyal for thinking that perhaps Wei talks about it a little too much. After all, the past is the past and while one can feel nostalgic, it seems to the maid that Wei prefers to live there, dwelling in her mind amid her lost glories as an imperial consort.

As Wei also frequently reminds the maid, she too was a maidservant before she became a great lady. She was at the court as a personal servant to one of the emperor's favourite consorts. This was a lady called Ban, a member of the much-envied group known as the *jieyu*. Wei's fresh-faced beauty did not go unnoticed by the lascivious emperor, and seeing the emperor's interest, the consort quickly offered her maid as a gift to her imperial master. Wei had a natural aptitude, both at being a courtesan and at navigating the tricky waters of court politics. She quickly made her way to the top tier of the court and soon became a *jieyu* consort herself, of equal status to her previous mistress. Her family were delighted by her meteoric rise, and expected that she would bring great honour to the family and their ancestors.

Sadly, it was not to be, for the fickle emperor quickly lost interest in her and turned his attention to younger girls at the court. His increasing depravity eventually led to his death – a death that left all his favoured consorts struggling to survive in a chaotic and perilous situation. Wei's diplomatic skills ensured that she was not among those who perished in the brutal infighting that followed the emperor's death, but she lacked the one vital card that would have allowed her to stay on at the court. She had never given the emperor a child, and because she lacked the status of mother to an infant of the imperial blood, there was no longer a place for Wei at the court.

Wei was sent to look after the mausoleum where the emperor had been buried – an ostensible honour that amounted in effect to banishment. It is now the thirteenth year of her exile and there are no signs that her situation will improve. 'Nobody in the court even remembers me, I suspect,' she used to joke bitterly to her maid, but now she rarely talks about even the possibility of reinstatement at court.

Wei pauses and turns around on the last step of the gate towers to look back at the earthen mound of the mausoleum where the emperor is buried. With a heavy sigh, she says to the maid, 'I wonder whether in his afterlife His Majesty enjoys beautiful sunsets as we have done today.'

The maid shuffles her feet uneasily, for she finds it unsettling when Wei is in one of these moods. 'Your Grace, let us go home now. It is getting dark and a little chilly,' she pleads, with concern in her voice. She wants to get her mistress off the grounds of the mausoleum and back to their small but well-appointed house, where Wei's melancholy usually clears away.

Perversely, Wei insists instead that they should go back down along the Spiritual Way to take a closer look at one of the sculptures. The sculptures are already weathering, but it now seems that some of the damaged ones have been repaired and reinstalled. Wei wants to check whether the workers have kept intact a crouching tiger that she particularly admires. The maid does not share Wei's curiosity, but where her mistress goes, she must follow, though she does so while casting uneasy glances at the ever-lengthening shadows around the tomb.

The maid is surprised at how speedily the statues have been repaired – in fact although Wei had noted the problem, she had not yet even reported it to the authorities. It is all rather strange – last year, when she reported that loose tiles were falling from the roof of the gate tower, the response was one of massive indifference.

'Some high officials must be scheduled to visit the mausoleum and the *qindian* Imperial Resting Palace,' comments Wei. Although her links to the court have been completely severed, the former courtesan well understands how it operates. She explains to the maid that in difficult times the emperor or other high officials will visit the imperial mausoleum, allegedly to reconnect with their imperial ancestors, but really as a way of publicly affirming their political legitimacy as members of the imperial dynasty.

Wei sighs, and the maid looks at her mistress with concern. She knows that Wei still nurses the forlorn hope that she might be noticed on one such visit, and that some official, or even the new emperor himself, might invite her back to court. However, even with her limited political experience, the maid knows that it is highly improbable that this momentous invitation will ever come. Her mistress has no royal descendants, and no rich or powerful relatives or friends to speak for her before the new emperor. To the current royal court, Wei is nothing, of no use to anyone. Nor is the maid too displeased about this, for though their exile can be lonely, it is safely distant from the intrigues and dangers of the imperial palace.

The maid watches as Wei gently touches the back of the crouching stone tiger and says, 'Do you remember the sculpted tiger we saw the other day outside His Resting Palace? The fluid lines on the back were so beautifully carved that you could almost imagine the stripes on the tiger's fur. And look at this one, so carelessly done! What can He think of it?' She yanks her hand away in disgust.

The maid does not ask whom her mistress means when she talks of 'He', or 'Him' – such references are always to the late emperor. So she does not say anything but stares at the sky, hoping that her mistress will notice that the stars are coming out and it is getting late. Wei asks, 'What date is it today?'

Mausoleum carers

Numerous consorts and court servants were sent to look after imperial mausoleums during the Han era. Although there were a few rare cases when someone volunteered to be a mausoleum carer, the majority were given their position as a form of banishment from court. For childless consorts, caring for their deceased emperor's mausoleum was considered a natural continuation of their chosen life. However, in some cases consorts who had given birth to imperial descendants would apply for permission to become a mausoleum carer for their deceased husband.

'It is the fourteenth, your grace,' the maid answers, though she has to turn her head back to do so, because she has already taken several steps in the direction she wishes they would go. It is getting dark and, like everyone who lives close to the mausoleum, the maid has heard the many ghost stories that collect about such a place. She very much does not want to stay around to discover if any of them are true.

The maid is relieved to see that Wei is absent-mindedly following her along the pathway, although painfully slowly. 'It is the full moon tomorrow and we are having the ceremony of the nightly display of His clothing and crown,' her mistress murmurs.

In the Resting Palace, daily, monthly and seasonal offerings are made to the deceased emperor. In the main pavilion, the emperor's clothing and crown are kept on an altar as if he were still alive. He still eats in the afterlife, so he is offered food four times a day. He still sleeps, so his bed is kept tidy and comfortable. On certain days of the year the emperor still meets his officials, and he is cleaned and dressed for the occasion. He is still the sovereign descended to the world as its ruler, so his clothing and crown are taken in a procession every month.

The maid does not like the Resting Palace. Every time she has to go within it, the decorative wooden animals on the walls seem alive, there seems to be a malevolent presence watching her, and the air is unnaturally cold. When she is in those haunted rooms, the maid is reminded of the 'love' story of the famous Emperor Wu and his beloved consort Wang, and of how, after Wang died, the Qi state warlock would call back her spirit in the dead of night so that he could see his beloved through a net curtain.

The maid covers her ears with her hands when this story is told.

The maid never met the deceased emperor while he was alive and feels no close connection to him, so she finds the whole business of meals and ceremonies both bizarre and absurd. But she knows that Wei, other consorts, and close maidservants who had served the emperor think that all this is perfectly natural, and they do as has been done for previous emperors in a tradition stretching back hundreds of years.

'Last month during the *Tailao* sacrifice, He was offered a whole roasted bull, wasn't He? Did you see them preparing the wheat yesterday?' Wei asks the maid. 'New wheat is for May,' she adds. The maid shakes her head and says nothing, clutching her robes about her to hide the fact that she is shivering gently, and not just because of the cool evening breeze.

'Don't be scared. None of those ghost stories people tell are true. I have been here for almost thirteen years. Have I ever encountered any ghosts? I wish I had, you know, so that

FORTY THOUSAND TERRACOTTA FIGURES WERE EXCAVATED AT THE BURIAL PIT OF HAN EMPEROR JINGDI (r. 157–141 BC)

I could meet Him again. Ghosts are not the problem, girl – living men can be far more horrible.' The maid knows that Wei is trying to comfort her, but she is making things worse. Sometimes her mistress seems to belong more among the dead than with the living.

Rather resentfully, the maid thinks that Wei has been very inconsiderate tonight, dallying in the gathering twilight of the mausoleum so that she can wallow in self-pity and the memory of her dead emperor.

'That man treated you so badly! Why would you hope to meet him again?' Usually the maid would never speak so directly to her mistress, but her good judgement has been warped by frustration and fear. The maid also knows that she is being irreverent towards the deceased emperor by not referring to him as 'His Majesty' in accordance with Wei's all-too-often repeated mantra, 'His Majesty is always His Majesty, whether he is dead or alive.'

Wei does not reply, and the maid says nothing more, for now they are finally meandering towards the exit of the mausoleum. As they step out through the eastern gate, Wei looks back yet again at the earthen mound where the emperor is buried. The gigantic mound reaches high into the twilight sky, a dark shape outlined against the first stars of the evening. (So large are the monumental mounds in Han imperial mausoleums that they have become distinctive features of the local landscape.) The maid sees Wei turn her gaze from the imperial mound to a smaller mound situated a short distance from the emperor's burial place and knows that Wei is looking at where her old mistress, the imperial consort Ban, sleeps in her eternal rest.

The present maid knows all about the woman whom Wei served as a maid. Of all the emperor's many consorts, Ban was the only one whom Wei truly respected and admired. Ban's knowledge was remarkable, and her virtue and integrity were unparalleled in the court. Wei tells the maid, 'Ban had the foresight to envision the ugly court infighting and the courage to escape from it before it destroyed her as well. She deserves to be buried where she is – beside the emperor. What will be my fate when I die?' This time it is Wei's turn to shiver in the early evening air.

The maid takes Wei's arm and almost drags her away from the gate. All they need now is to make a left turn and walk north to their home. After the sombre quiet of the mausoleum compound, the street outside feels bustling and slightly chaotic. Although it is almost dark, the life of an ordinary town goes on; people meet and talk, eat and drink, work and sleep, living their lives in the present.

Wei and her maid pass a small group of night guards getting ready for their shift and see an elderly couple carrying a batch of timber, probably returning home after their work of the day. The pair turn into a small house, and the sound of family greetings and conversation spills briefly into the street.

The maid asks Wei, 'Do you miss having a normal life?'

'Normal? What is normal? I certainly envy that elderly couple who just passed us by. When you are old there's nothing better than having a spouse for comfort and company.' Wei seems to have pulled herself out of her dark mood, but she looks a bit lost. From the day she went to the court as a maidservant to her endless days as a mausoleum carer, her life has changed dramatically and her social status has risen high and tumbled down, but her fate has always been the same – it is and forever will be subjugated to the needs of her emperor, even after his death.

Before they reach home Wei is to receive another reminder of the reality of her fate. They are passing by the *yiguandao* (Avenue of Cloth and Crown), the road reserved for sacred processions, where workmen are digging a pit. It looks as though they are preparing an elaborate grave.

Wei stops and stares. What are these men doing that is so urgent they have to dig a pit through the night? She asks one of them, who looks as though he might be the supervisor, and the man tells her that the minister of agriculture is critically ill and the workmen are preparing his burial ground. The maid notes that the supervisor is gazing at Wei with a peculiar expression, as though he has seen her before but for the moment cannot place exactly who she is.

'I can't believe what you are saying! How can you do this? Don't you know that this is a reserved space where His Majesty's cloth and crown are carried in procession? This is sacred ground. How dare you ruin it!' Wei's voice starts to rise to a hysterical pitch.

'Which Majesty are you talking about exactly? Because the Majesty who lives in the royal palace has granted this land, as an honour, to the minister of agriculture,' the supervisor states with authority.

The maid does not know what to do. She knows that the world has moved on after the old emperor's death, and she accepts the changes, but Wei lives in her own world, a world that ceased to exist over a decade ago. This is not the first time she has seen Wei get into hopeless arguments with mausoleum guards and others. The mausoleum and the courtyard of the Resting Palace are not the holy, untouchable sites they once were. The tombs of the local residents and of high governmental officials encroach more and more upon land that was once part of the mausoleum grounds. The maid can see the increasing dilapidation of the Resting Palace and other parts of the mausoleum; the grass growing through the pavilion floors and the altars covered in dust. Soon the mausoleum will be almost forgotten, but she knows that Wei turns a blind eye to it all, seeing only the mausoleum and grounds as they were in their original lonely splendour.

'Your Grace, come away, please, let us go home now.' There is no way of stopping the crew of grave diggers, so the maid finally succeeds in dragging Wei away, but her mistress turns to look back as they resume their walk home together. The supervisor has heard the maid address Wei as 'Your Grace' and gestures for them to stop. The maid keeps Wei walking, and after a few moments the supervisor lets them go.

'Did you see that? He almost recognized me,' Wei tells the maid, with the ghost of a wistful smile on her face.

Three ritual ceremonies

Three types of ritual ceremonies were held at Han imperial mausoleums on a daily and seasonal basis. First, four meals were offered to the deceased king in the Resting Palace and these four meals resembled those the emperor would have had when he was alive. Second, the prime minister would sometimes be sent by the court to preside over seasonal ceremonies and to make offerings in the deceased emperor's mausoleum. Third, every month the deceased emperor's clothing and crown were taken from the Resting Palace and put on a cart for a procession around the mausoleum compound. This ceremony was normally presided over by the *Taichang* (Grand Master of Ceremonies) and attended by other officials.

戌 THIRD HOUR OF
THE NIGHT
(20.00–21.00: SECOND PART OF *XU*)

THE SCRIBE COMES
TO A DECISION

*Explore the relationship between heaven and humans,
discern the pattern of ancient and modern changes, and
formulate your own view of history.*

Autobiography of the Grand Historian, Sima Qian (145–*c.* 86 BC)

The flame of the table lamp casts a shadowy pattern
onto the archive shelves and throws the flickering
shadows onto the crumbling plaster of the faded white
wall behind. It is like reading the cracks on a divination bone,
but the dim, dancing shapes are too mobile for Liu to form a
prediction. Through the narrow window the refreshing smell
of Osmanthus blossom wafts into the room from the garden
outside. The occasional chirp from a sleepy bird signals that the
day is drawing to an end and settling into a pleasant evening.
But Liu's mind is hardly as calm as the evening. Turbulent
thoughts tumble around in his head and trouble his soul, as his
mind grapples with horrible news.

Yang, a fellow scribe working in the imperial court has been brutally beheaded, paying with his life for placing into the official record an account of the crown prince's improper behaviour. The prince had molested a senior maid-in-waiting, who later committed suicide out of shame. When Yang's report made this misconduct public, the infuriated and frightened crown prince had literally called for Yang's head. The execution was staged outside the royal pavilion with selected scribes in attendance to observe the salutary lesson.

Of course the matter did not end there – rather than silencing his annoying critic, the crown prince has ensured that everyone now knew what he had done. There were rumours swirling around the palace that the emperor himself was now taking a personal interest in the case, not least because his appointed successor has demonstrated a worrying lack of judgement.

Yang's death might seem an absurd and unnecessary martyrdom to many people, but it all sounds tragically natural to Liu and other fellow scribes. Their job is to keep the records, and if the records lie, or omit inconvenient truths, then what are scribes but second-rate storytellers? Yet in these times, as Yang's fate has so grotesquely demonstrated, a scribe who does his job properly does so at the risk of his life.

Han scribes such as Yang, and Liu himself, are greatly esteemed for their integrity, and part of their prestige comes from the fact that they keep the records without fear or favour. Yet change is sweeping aside the old traditions and social values, especially when these values clash with the needs of the imperial bureaucracy. Powerful emperors such as Wu (156–87 BC) insist that history is whatever they say it is, and many scribes who have tried to maintain the purity of their records have died tragically as a result. Yet still, brave scribes such as Yang keep trying, for just as a warrior might wield his sword in defence of a hopeless cause, a scholar fights with his pen and, like a warrior, he might win fame but at the cost of his life.

In the dim twilight Liu's face grows solemn as he remembers when he and Yang together studied Confucian rites and writing. Both were praised by their teachers for their courage, righteousness and incorruptible natures, but it was always Yang who was most committed to their craft. Liu used to envy Yang, who was from a prestigious family of scribes. In their small, interconnected circle, the scion of such a family needed only a modicum of competence to be guaranteed a good job for life. Yet Yang was more than merely competent – he was bright, excellent at his craft, well-connected and likeable.

After their education Liu chose to be a *Lingshi* scribe, working under the *Yushi* Grand Sector, one of the most important and powerful bureaucratic officials in the Han court. Liu is based at *Lantai*, the Orchard Pavilion, where the emperor's decrees, official government reports and memoranda, state laws and maps are archived. Liu's offices are close to the Shiquge library, which is just behind the grand Weiyang palace, so Liu takes the chance to visit the library's impressive book collection whenever he has the time.

His old schoolfriend Yang went to work at the court as a *Taishi* scribe, responsible for the documentation of affairs of state and the details of royal business. Despite his prestigious position and the wide consensus that he had a bright future, Yang was always somewhat pessimistic. He knew that no matter how high his status, a scribe can fall from favour overnight and be executed the following day. When they met, Yang would frequently remind Liu of the historic tragedy of the *Taishi* scribe family of Qi state.

Three courageous scribes, Bo and his two brothers, Zhong and Shu, had lost their lives for their courageous attempts to record the scandalous behaviour of a high-ranking official and the wife of one of his senior officers. And that, Yang would soberly point out, was during the 'Spring-and-Autumn' period (770–476 BC), when scribes had much more licence than they have today.

Now Liu wonders what role the story of Bo, Zhong and Shu played in Yang's tragic death. Did the events of the past simply foreshadow Yang's own fate, or did the deaths of his principled predecessors inspire Yang to follow the path they had taken?

Liu thinks sadly of another of Yang's favourite maxims: 'If the lips are gone, the teeth will be cold.' By attacking the scribes, the state damages itself, since it is very much in the interest of the state that the scribes keep accurate records. Of course, many high officials support the integrity of reports in general, but still violently insist on an exception being made for a particular case (their own), and consequently the work of a scribe is a fine balancing act that has dangers never imagined by outsiders.

On the desk before Liu, there is a small burner on which two large characters, 'Cang Jie', have been written on the belly in beautiful script. Cang Jie, the legendary inventor of writing, is commonly worshipped by those in the profession as the God of Scribes. Liu remembers well the day when his father took him to visit Cang Jie's temple. In dramatically exaggerated tones, Liu's father had told the young Liu how Cang Jie invented the art of writing after careful observation of the stars, the patterns of a turtle's shell, and the lines of a feather, and thereafter by studying the shapes of mountains and rivers.

On the day when Liu was preparing to depart to take up his position in the imperial court, his father had taken up that burner and with bold, vigorous strokes shaped by years of experience he had written 'Cang Jie' in black ink on it. He had said to Liu, 'I don't expect you to become the head of scribes anytime soon, but I do hope you will always have the courage to confront wrongdoing and the strength to see you through the difficulties that confrontation causes.'

Even before he started formal training, Liu had received rigorous instruction on calligraphy from his father and now, after years of practice, his brush strokes have become almost as forceful. Liu looks at the burner, really seeing it for the first time in years. He notes that the Cang Jie characters on the coarse surface are faded and blurring at the edges where the ink has been absorbed into the porous pottery. Liu absent-mindedly picks up a brush pen and dips its head into an inkwell on the desk, and while he brushes the thick dark ink over his father's writing, he recalls the debates and discussions he used to have with his father while he was still alive.

Once, Liu was reading the case of a land dispute between a rich landlord and his tenant that had ended with the assassination of the former and the execution of the latter. He raised the case with his father, and they began to discuss whether the state should have a monopoly on social justice. This was, of course, an issue that Liu would not dare to discuss with anyone else, since the official position was that the state's enforcement of justice was infallible and not to be questioned.

Somehow Liu cannot bring himself to believe this, for he has a sneaking suspicion that sometimes the state itself is corrupt and wrong. His father, when this was put to him, told Liu that others have occasionally challenged the state's authority. On his travels, Liu's father had been to many parts of the country, including places where not the state, but local elders and councils have the decisive role in maintaining social order and justice. Liu's father reckoned that as scribes it was their job to report and record such different approaches to maintaining social order – despite the dangers of doing so.

'The Grand Historian Siam Qian,' quoted Liu's father, 'said in his *Records of the Grand Historian*: those scholars who are restricted by their specialized knowledge and who hold to rigid principles are isolated from ordinary people. They are a different breed to those who obtain honour and distinction by compromising their beliefs. We scribes should take this lesson to heart.'

Now, after the news of Yang's death, Liu thinks again of the many questions that he never had time to discuss with his father. What is fame? Is dying for one's principles more important than life itself? Was Yang's death heroic or unnecessary – and who is Liu, that he should pass judgement in any case?

Abruptly, Liu stands up and walks out of the room to get some fresh air. He lives in a relatively quiet section of the court in an area set aside for low-ranking in-house officers. Their shared courtyard is a considerable distance from the more ostentatious part of the palace – something for which Liu is always grateful. Standing in the middle of the courtyard, Liu gazes at the sky above.

Astrological calculations are not a part of the duties of a *Lingshi* scribe, but Liu enjoys observing the changing pattern of the heavens and making predictions for his own personal use. However, the courtyard's view is confined by the high walls to a limited square of sky, and the moon is covered by clouds. In his mood of foreboding, Liu wonders if the hidden light foreshadows something uncertain and sinister.

He smiles ruefully, recalling that his father, a follower of Confucius, was not very supportive of his enthusiasm for astrological predictions and the Huang-Lao (Yellow Emperor and Laosi) doctrine. 'Sky signs' his father called them dismissively, arguing that astrology teaches nothing about the interactions of the past with the future. In the end, Liu has taught himself what he knows of astrology by reading through the archives and records now available to him in his role as a scribe.

Deciding that his limited view of the heavens leaves little space for prognostications, Liu returns with some disappointment to his rooms. It is getting chilly outside, so he puts his hands around the base of his lamp to warm himself, and as he does so he notes that his thoughts have been so much in turmoil that he still has not attended to the governmental report that lies waiting, half-folded, in the middle of his desk.

The document was delivered earlier today, and since it is from a senior scribe it really should be ready for tomorrow. Liu forces himself to focus on this task and lays the scroll fully open. The scroll has ten slips, which are knotted together evenly with a hemp thread, so when spread out the document takes up almost half of the space on his small desk.

Liu checks the text carefully right down the entire length of the scroll. Both his father and his schooling have given Liu an extensive knowledge of the numerous characters of different types of script, and this hard-won expertise was instrumental in getting him his current job. Yet there are thousands of characters yet to be mastered, and Liu continues to learn more and more of them at the Shiquge library, where he receives instruction from some of the top scholars of the state.

Liu is now familiar with the six writing styles officially recognized by the Han court, including difficult ones such as the 'insect' style. But like his father before him, he has concentrated on mastering the *li* clerical script, for this is the most common style of official documents in the court. Liu needs to check that the document before him is not only accurate in content, but also beautifully written and with a consistent style. 'A standardized yet beautifully written document testifies to the imperial authority and the seriousness and professionalism of our imperial bureaucracy,' Liu was informed when he first arrived to work at the court.

Liu frowns as he notes that two characters on the second slip of his scroll are crudely written and poorly aligned, a fault not only ugly in itself, but one that lowers the quality of the rest of the scroll. Liu tuts to himself as he scrapes the offending characters off the page and rewrites them, carefully matching his style with the rest of the scroll. It looks suspiciously as if this document was written by a beginner who was taking dictation from his superior. Where this unskilled scribe had forgotten how to write certain characters, he had evidently left blank spaces that he had filled in later. The end result was poor spacing and sloppy lettering that left a general impression of either haste or ineptitude.

Liu does what he can, and rectifies a few more errors, corrects some very non-standard character forms, and afterwards very carefully checks whether the figures so hastily jotted down express the values they are supposed to. Properly recording numbers is where accuracy often fails, especially with dictation taken down in haste. Liu well recalls a recent case in which a report to the emperor had meant to state 'ten' but had mistakenly stated 'a hundred'. Since the report had been from a top official at the royal mint, this discrepancy was severe enough to result in a flogging for the minister, with additional punishments for the original writer of the report and for the scribe who had failed to spot the error.

When he has finished with the text, Liu rolls up the scroll and puts it carefully back on the shelf for delivery tomorrow.

He realizes that working has done nothing to assuage his simmering resentment at the death of Yang, so he reaches into a beautifully engraved bamboo box by his desk and pulls out a text at random. He has recently borrowed from the Shiquge archives the *Zuo Zhuan* ('The Zuo Tradition', written by one of the most famous scribe scholars, Zuo Qiuming, *c.* 502–422 BC; a narrative chronicle of the Spring-and-Autumn Annals), and he hopes that reading one of these classical works from the Confucius canon will ease his mind.

While official documents use longer bamboo slips, these texts are shorter and (Liu notes critically), often better written. The volume he unfolds tells the story of Duke Jing of Jin State (died 581 BC). With admirably succinct and straightforward prose, the blind scribe Zuo Qiuming had described this once-powerful ruler's often bizarre life, and even more bizarre death. While reading, Liu marvels that the authorities of the time had allowed Zuo to give the facts, including the duke's slaughter of a powerful witch who had the temerity to predict his death. As it happened, the duke died at the predicted time by drowning ignominiously in the toilet – all of which Zuo reported, with not just the facts uncensored but also his own candid and unflattering opinions.

The Great Historian Sima Qian

Siam Qian was born to a well-known, prestigious family of scribes. His father, Sima Tan (second century BC–110 BC) was the *Taishi* scribe for Emperor Wu, and in charge of reporting on matters of astrology and the calendar. On his deathbed, Sima Tan told his son to continue his unfinished project of writing the *Jizhuanti*-style general history of China (a style of history presented as a series of biographies).

Sima Qian inherited his father's position in the court, but he soon offended the emperor by speaking out in support of the general, Li Ling, who had been captured by the Xiongnu in his unsuccessful campaign. As punishment for his boldness in disagreeing with his emperor, Sima Qian was castrated. He endured this horrible humiliation and continued to work on the general history that his father had charged him with completing.

Sima Qian's innovative magnum opus, *Records of the Grand Historian*, set the framework for later historical works, with the liberal perspective of the text followed by scholars and literati of later ages. His unparalleled literary value is praised by Lu Xun (1881–1936), a twentieth-century Chinese literary giant, as 'the historian's most perfect song, a *Li Sao* [translated as 'Encountering Sorrow', a renowned Chinese poem written during the Warring States period] without the rhyme'.

With a heavy heart Liu replaces the slip into its box. Long gone are the days of the 'Spring-and-Autumn' and 'Warring States' periods when scribes such as Zuo could criticize with impunity their rulers' wrongdoings and threaten them with the judgement of posterity.

Liu walks out into the courtyard again, but this time, instead of seeking the hidden stars in the clouded heavens, he looks down at the flagstones where the shed petals from the Osmanthus tree cover the ground. Soon the wind will blow the petals away and nobody will notice, or even remember that they were there. In much the same way, Liu can bend to the dictates of the imperial court, do his work and become a forgotten functionary, swept away and forgotten by history. Or he can make a stand, and die memorably for something worthwhile. At that moment Liu decides that Yang's bravery and the heavy price he paid will not be forgotten, for he himself will carry on Yang's work.

亥 FOURTH HOUR OF THE NIGHT

(21.00–22.00 FIRST PART OF *HAI*)

THE PERFORMER FINISHES HER ACT

As Nan dances in the centre of the hall for her aristocratic audience, back at home her sister is at this moment bringing a new child into the world. An elderly maid-in-waiting had brought the news while Nan was preparing for the evening's performance. Her sister's waters had broken and the birth was imminent. So now Nan wants nothing more than to rush to her sister's side, but she is the lead performer for tonight's gathering. It would have been an unthinkable insult to her host if she were to leave suddenly, not to mention the chaos into which her departure would throw the rest of her troupe.

Unlike many other entertainers who sell themselves to the court, Nan has some freedom as a member of a private troupe of performers for a high-ranking aristocrat. Nevertheless, she is usually expected to stay at her employer's palace for the duration of her contract unless – as tonight – she is called on to perform at other places, such as this royal hall.

So now Nan dances, and tries not to think of what is happening at her sister's home, for she knows that she cannot dance properly while she is distracted. This is not merely a matter of putting on a superlative show for the audience – a distracted dancer is a dancer who makes mistakes, and a mistake can lead to the sort of injury that might prevent Nan from performing just at the moment when her family is going to need the extra money.

Already there have been a few awful moments when she almost fell while flinging out her long sleeves as she bent into a complex series of moves. At such moments she fakes a smile to cover her little flaws, and judging by the applause from her aristocratic audience no one has noticed her small wobbles. Yet the applause from the noblemen lounging at their ease does not put Nan's mind at rest – instead she feels aggrieved that she must perform for them while she would much rather be at her sister's side.

Yet Nan's sister certainly understands and even approves of what Nan is doing, for the sisters are the current generation of a long line of performers. They came originally from the Huai River region, an area well known for its entertaining performances. The dancers became fashionable once the emperor began promoting performers from the region, and they are now much in demand in aristocratic circles in the capital, Chang'an. To take advantage of their new popularity Nan's family moved years ago to Chang'an seeking employment, fame, and of course, prosperity.

Now retired, Nan's aunt was the first to appear in the royal court, for she had a beautiful voice and was already famous as a singer of the lyrical Chu songs popular with the Han dynasty. Nan is one of only two girls in the family's second generation, so almost from birth she was destined to be a court performer, and she grew up with the weight of the family's reputation on her slender shoulders. When Nan was a little girl, her aunt began teaching her to sing and play different musical instruments, but while Nan proved a competent singer and musician, it quickly became clear that she was not up to the superlative standard required for a performer at the imperial court.

Yet what she lacks in musical ability Nan makes up for in flexibility and athleticism. Given her natural grace and petite frame it quickly became clear to the family that Nan should train as a drum dancer. Drum dancing is difficult to master, but it allows for a lot of individual interpretation by the dancer. From her father's dance routine Nan picked up the steps used by acrobats and contemporary male dancers, blending these more masculine moves into her natural light-footed style.

From her mother she learned the very different moves of the feminine dance, in which the dancer uses her long, flowing sleeves to maximum effect, hurling them up and out, pulling, shaking, twisting and towing them to create a sinuous cloak of colour that swirls about her body as she turns her waist and legs. Her training made her into an all-around dancer, but it was rigorous and continual. When Nan is now praised for her exquisite performances, only her parents know how far she has come and how much she has suffered for her craft. Finally, at the age of sixteen, she went to the court as a *yueji* performer, and quickly made her name as a dancer.

So now she dances, her long, narrow, sleeves flaring out in elegant, curling lines from her waist and chest as she flies across the stage like a nimble fairy. The musicians, standing and kneeling in the corridor, belt out the last sounds from their chime bells and the *qing* music stone, and the drummer rolls a final crescendo on his drums.

This is the signal for Nan to end her dance, which she does with a difficult final move, stepping out from the middle of the hall, then rushing to one side, pumping her legs as she suddenly

**EARTHENWARE FIGURE OF A DANCER DEPICTING
THE TRADITIONAL LONG FLOWING SLEEVES THAT
PLAYED A KEY PART IN THEIR PERFORMANCE**

leaps forward. At the same time, her body bends backwards quickly as she flings her long sleeves upwards. The party-goers stop their drinking and merry chatter to burst into an ovation, but Nan does not stop to bow or recognize this honour. Instead, she brushes aside the light, yellowish silk curtain and walks quietly into the corridor, slightly out of breath, and with sweat pouring down her cheeks.

The other performers look with concern at her pale face and colourless cheeks that are usually flushed after such a strenuous routine. In the small community of the dance troupe, word has quickly gone around about her sister's pregnancy, and Nan knows that the others are concerned, but also worried that distraction might affect her performance that evening. They know better than to disturb her, though, for Nan has only a few moments to rally herself before her next display.

The aroma wafting from a nearby incense burner calms the girl down a little, and she tries to slow her breathing with deep, even breaths, but her excitement at becoming an aunt remains, mixed with concern for her sister. Nan bites her lip, warning herself to control her eagerness for the performance to be done. Has the child been born already? Are mother and infant both well? And what if they are not? Here inside the palace, so far from home, Nan feels a flutter of panic at the thought of losing her only sibling and true friend.

Suddenly, from the centre of the hall come chords of bleak music. The agony of the song resonates perfectly with Nan's sudden fear. The singer steps into the hall to perform and Nan listens intently from behind the curtain, following the music, and now certain that something has gone wrong for her sister. She wishes the song was not so sad, but on the other hand, knowing that the writer shares her feelings of sorrow and desperation brings some comfort to this lonely situation in a hall far from home.

It also helps to know that even the great are afflicted by the sadness she feels. The founding emperor of the Han dynasty, Liu Bang, came from Chu state and was very fond of Chu songs. He wrote the *Dafeng* Song ('Song of a Strong Gale') upon returning to his hometown and meeting with old acquaintances after he unified the country and became the emperor. In the song, the emperor tearfully asks the audience how he can find warriors courageous enough to protect his empire.

This bleak, doleful style of Chu songs has been adopted by the singers in the Han court. Many emperors and empresses were themselves great songwriters and singers. Powerful as the Emperor Wu (157–87 BC) had been, he still composed the song 'Ode of Autumn Wind' to express the peculiar kind of melancholy derived from joy.

The musicians play on the *se* (plucked zither), the *pipa* (Chinese lute) and *fou* (ceramic instrument), and the chime bells ring out the harmonious, penetrating notes of the *zheng* tonal scale. 'My family married me to a place beneath another corner of the sky,' the singer recites, singing the first line slowly.

This is the famous 'Song of Sorrow'. The widely circulated song was written by Wusun, a Han princess who was married by Emperor Wu to a *Kunmi* king in the far north-west of the empire. It was a diplomatic marriage, so no one felt it mattered that the youthful princess was married to an aged husband. Lonely and homesick, the princess wrote the song to express the overwhelming isolation and cultural deprivation she felt. 'I have been delivered to the king of a foreign country. I live in a house with a simple banner wall and a domed roof. Meat is my food and milk my drink. Living in this way makes my heart ache. If I were a yellow swan, I could fly back to my homeland.'

The singer finishes the first stanza on a high pitch. The way she sings the last word of the song exactly resembles how Nan's mother and aunt performed the same song, with that prolonged, sharp tone punctuating the end verse.

'You have to take your time and never rush,' her aunt always used to say. Everyone is moved by the singer's sonorous performance, perfectly matched with the instrumental accompaniment. The song successfully transported them to the far-off foreign land where the princess Wusun had lived, even though few people were familiar with the princess's tragic life. The song, however, spoke powerfully to Nan's current predicament. She too is trapped in a situation where the court is the insurmountable obstacle between her and her beloved sister.

A guest, inspired by the music, steps into the hall and starts singing the same stanza. Those seated on the floor around him join in and the atmosphere in the room suddenly becomes more solemn. The guests stop eating and drinking, and some even find tears welling in their eyes and coursing freely down their cheeks.

The host is pleased with this outburst of emotion for it means that his guests are being properly entertained that evening. But he does not want the mood to become overly sentimental so he nods at the singer, signalling for her to leave quietly, while he waves a hand to the group of waiting musicians in the corridor, gesturing for them to play something rousing and cheerful.

Nan looks for her cousin Dong among the musicians as they prepare their next piece. Nan and Dong are very fond of each other, but neither of them is brave enough to express their love. Even though they work in the same palace, they don't often see each other privately. And unlike Nan, Dong has freedom to go in and out of the palace. *Does he know my sister is giving birth? Should I try and ask him to send a message home?* Nan wonders. She sees him looking at her and the eye contact gives her some comfort.

Now the beating of drums and the din and roar of stone, bamboo and bronze instruments suddenly fills the room, as if, all of a sudden, the audience has been transported to the middle of a busy, bustling market. Two servants quickly lay out large plates and drums in a circle on the floor and a small group of dancers enter the hall like a school of fish, each following the other in a flash of dazzling colour. Nan is on again, about to lead the closing session of the evening's entertainment, a complicated dance involving plates and drums. In this, one of the most popular dances of the time, dancers jump between plates and drums to showcase their dance and acrobatic skills.

CERAMIC VESSELS SHOWING ACROBATS BALANCING ON THE RIMS

Originally, only around six or seven plates and drums were used, but to satisfy the aristocrats' ever-growing madness for display and competition, the number of both is now sometimes over twenty. This challenges the dancers, pushing them to the very limits of their coordination and skill, and because this is a very physically demanding exercise, the dancers also need to keep careful control of their breathing. During rehearsals that afternoon, three young, inexperienced dancers had crashed into each other, earning a beating from the instructor for their carelessness.

Nan starts first with a solo dance. On her tiptoes she holds a silk banner that she waves high above her head as she pivots on the floor towards the drums. She then rotates herself on and around the drums, and then quickly jumps lightly up and over them, lifting both legs high off the ground so that her light cotton dress and silk banner flutter gracefully in the air behind her. Briefly, she stands on one drum, deftly steps onto another placed slightly off-centre, and then jumps around and between them gracefully.

She is a dancing dragon, a flying bird as her supple body moves around the stage while her sleeves cross beautifully in the air above her head and her silk banner floats and billows like clouds gathering about a mountaintop. She is supposed to keep a subtle smile on her face while she performs this routine, but tonight she just can't manage it. Fortunately, her suppressed worry and excitement somehow feeds into all her moves and the flow of her clothing, and this, together with the music, blends with the atmosphere of the evening. The guests are so intoxicated by the dance that none of them notices the other dancers standing in the outer circle about to join her.

A male dancer steps onto the stage. He bends down and puts his feet, knees and one hand on five drums and plates. Two other dancers move a shelf in front of him. With his left hand, he beats a drum hanging from the shelf – a dramatic change of pace that startles the guests from their reverie. They laugh nervously and settle back to enjoy the coming acrobatic display.

While the acrobats take over the space in the middle of the hall, Nan leads the female dancers to a narrower space outside the main performance area. She pairs up with a young female dancer on one side and another pair of dancers stand opposite them. They then dance in perfect synchronicity, with moves coordinated through long practice. The four begin by standing still and only gently waving their hands. Then, they lift one hand from their sides and whip the other down on the other side, following this by flinging both arms wide expansively.

Their fabric sleeves swing like willow branches swaying softly in a gentle spring breeze in a continuous wave of colourful floating fabric that flies over the tops of their heads in the confined space. Some flying sleeves even brush against the guests who are sitting right in front of them, and the host is so moved that he stands and begins to imitate the flowing movements of the young dancers.

The dancers turn their faces to the guests and simultaneously gently gyrate their hips and legs. Their performances very often end with a flirtatious gesture, and this is certainly the case tonight. Nan and her partner extend one foot towards the guests and each bends over the outstretched leg at a 90-degree angle while stretching back the other leg. Nan's symmetrical body posture then gives way to her next solo dance as the others quietly step away.

Nan half squats, with her outstretched arms waving rhythmically to maintain her balance. She then turns her head sideways to look at her assistant. This helps a bit, as she does not wish her face to show her turbulent emotions to the guests this evening. The assistant places a plate next to her and she steps on it with one petite foot, lifts her other leg to the level of her waist, wing-tip shoe pointing straight ahead, and leans her upper body forward. She stands there with her foot outstretched, like a dragonfly perched tentatively on a reed, and holds this pose to deservedly win another ovation.

The guests are all crowding around the host as Nan slips offstage, and there is obvious envy at how well tonight's performance has gone. Some guests even ask about Nan and for the names of some of the other dancers. The moment could be a golden opportunity for some of the younger and more ambitious members of the troupe, for an aristocrat's patronage can lead to a meteoric rise in their careers. Male acrobats might become the lead performers in a royal or aristocratic court, while female dancers can find that aristocratic favour may lead to many things, not all of which are dance-related.

The (in)famous dancer Feiyan Zhao

Feiyan Zhao (45–1 BC) was abandoned immediately after her birth by her family, who were house slaves. She survived exposure in the wild for three days before she was found and adopted. She learned how to dance in Princess Yang'e's palace and became well known for her light dancing style, a combination of the flying swallow and phoenix. She was discovered by the Emperor Cheng when he visited the princess's palace and was admitted to the imperial court. Feiyan Zhao's sister Zhaoyi (alternatively named Hede) came into the court soon after, and the pair became the emperor's favourite consorts.

They became heavily involved in court politics and one of their most significant political acts was to help Xin Liu become the crown prince. Tragically, immediately after the death of Emperor Cheng, high court officials forced Zhaoyi Zhao to kill herself. Feiyan Zhao was better protected and for a while she retained her powerful status under the new emperor (Xin Liu). Eventually, though, Zhao's political base crumbled under a series of fierce attacks by rivals and enemies. Zhao was in effect exiled by being sent to look after Emperor Cheng's mausoleum, and there she eventually killed herself.

Doubtless some in Nan's troupe will become concubines, as many a dancer has done before, although history shows that this does not necessarily end well in every case. Life as a newcomer in a rich and powerful family is seldom easy or peaceful. Yet for some of the young, unsophisticated country girls the prospect of fame and fortune dangling so tantalizingly close is irresistible, and many are determined to seize the opportunity and deal with the consequences later.

The host rewards the musicians and performers with gold, small gifts and tokens, and as lead dancer Nan gets a particularly generous bonus – her gratuity is an elaborate jade ring. Everybody is brimming over with smiles and delight at a successful performance and its bountiful rewards. Yet, turning from the others, Nan thinks only of her sister and of how soon she can get away to greet her new niece or nephew.

(22.00–23.00: SECOND PART OF *HAI*)

THE ROYAL MAID PREPARES A BATH

When the princess returns to the royal palace, Bao knows that her mistress will want to take a bath. As the chief maid-in-waiting to Her Highness, it's Bao's job to know what her mistress wants without needing to be told. She has been doing this for five years now, staying attentive from dawn to late in the evening, and sometimes all night also – as she had to do recently when the princess was ill. Late evenings such as this one, while she waits for the princess to return from a banquet, are almost routine. For Bao, it is compensation enough that the princess trusts her completely and relies on her for almost everything.

Most of the afternoon was spent preparing the princess for the banquet – naturally, a royal daughter can never look less than perfect. Bao spent hours helping her lady put on her make-up, then brushing and arranging her thick, dark hair into an elaborate bun, and finally pinning the elaborate hairstyle in place with ebony combs. Then there was the tricky yet enjoyable task of selecting and preparing exactly the right jewellery to complement the highly elaborate gown that she and the princess had between them selected for the evening's occasion. Finally, Bao had placed a matching robe around her mistress's shoulders and knelt to ease expensive and delicate shoes onto her feet.

There was a palpable air of relief when the immaculately prepared princess had safely departed in their carriage three hours ago. Bao does not know, or care to know, the occasion for which the state banquet was being held. It is enough that she has sent her princess to the dinner properly prepared, and that she is ready to receive her royal charge properly once the princess returns.

First, proper lighting. Mentally calculating the time available, Bao goes to a side room next to the antechamber in the front yard. As the Lu state king's favourite daughter, the princess receives all kinds of luxurious gifts from her benevolent father and his relatives. She is particularly fond of lamps with artistic shapes, and accordingly she is often gifted lamps of exquisite craftsmanship, often made from exotic materials. There are enough of these lamps to have their own special storeroom, and after a quick survey of the shelves, Bao selects a goose-shaped bronze lamp. The princess once said that the design of this lamp conveys a unique sense of peace and relaxation.

This lamp was a birthday present from the princess's grandmother last year, and while no art expert, Bao appreciates the clever design that depicts a goose turning its head back to bite a fish with its beak. There is a lamp panel in the fish's belly, and underneath that a hollow space for water. When the lamp is lit, the water traps the smoke and prevents it from spreading out into the room where it would otherwise imbue an ineradicable smell into the delicate silks and fine linens. The lower half of the lamp is covered with fine fabric. It will offer a pleasing sight for the princess as she prepares for her bath, so Bao takes it upstairs and lights the wick within the fish's belly.

**A painted bronze lamp in the shape of
a goose holding a fish**

A warm flickering light fills the room, bringing to life the intricate details carved on the feathers of the goose's wings.

The bathroom is linked to the princess's bedroom by a connecting corridor. This corridor is dark as Bao steps inside, so she pauses to light the wicks in two ceramic dishes set into niches in the walls. Even though few palace servants are allowed into the royal bedchambers, Bao finds it annoying that no one had been available to light these lamps, and makes a note to follow up the matter later.

The bathroom is empty when she gets there, but there's no shortage of light. In fact the room is so bright that she stands blinking as her vision adjusts from the gloomy corridor. The light comes from a three-layered ceramic candelabra made in three parts. There is a base decorated with lively animals, a central stem, and three layers of lamp panels. The light radiates in multiple directions through the swan-like panels. Bao considers it a major perk of her job that although such beautiful objects are designed to please the princess, she gets to appreciate them too.

A few years ago, the princess used to bathe in a large bronze basin. Afterwards, the maids-in-waiting would have to carry away the used bathwater and dispose of it through drains outside the bathroom. As the princess grew older, the court decided to renovate her bathroom with a new bath set into the floor.

While not enormous, especially compared to the one the queen uses, it is still a substantial bath. There is a brick pavement around the edge with reliefs of plants and animals stamped onto the bricks. These reliefs are decorative (the princess likes to doodle a finger along the outlines as she bathes), but the rough patterns also provide traction on a surface that can get slippery when wet.

Bao frowns at a few leaves scattered on the bricks, and brushes them away, wondering how they had got there in the first place. Otherwise the space around the bath looks neat – as it should. Bao and the other maids had spent some considerable time cleaning the bath yesterday, washing traces of mud from some corner bricks and polishing the others. There's also something of a problem with the drainage system. The girls no longer have to carry out the waste water, but the porcelain pipes are not doing a good job of channelling it away. The water drains too slowly, and, kneeling to listen, Bao is not happy with the noises coming through the floor. Something else to report to the steward, she thinks with annoyance.

Now she pokes her head through a doorway at the back of the bathroom. There's a small furnace here, and two of the junior maids are boiling water. 'The princess is not back yet. Top up the pot with some cold water, and don't pour it into the bath until I say.' She returns to the bathroom proper to continue her preparations.

On a low platform in one corner is a lacquer *lian* (bathroom box) and a bamboo *si* (hamper). Cotton towels and some dried herbs are neatly placed inside the hamper. Bao selects a few spiced herbs and puts them into a *boshan* (incense burner). The pleasant aroma of the burning herbs immediately spreads through the room. The smoke creates a slight mist that helps to create a relaxing atmosphere, which Bao thinks will please the princess.

The next step is to warm the room. There's a proper furnace that supplies heat in winter, but that's not in use now, and in the early spring, draughts can get chilly. When the princess

THIS BRONZE INCENSE BURNER TAKES THE SHAPE
OF A MOUNTAIN. DIETIES AND MYTHICAL BEASTS
ROAM FREELY AMONG THE MIST AND CLOUDS

complained about this, Bao arranged for a portable furnace to be brought in, and now she summons a junior maid to stack the charcoal within. This close to the return of the princess, she does not want to dirty her own hands by doing the job herself. She carefully instructs the junior maid, showing her how to lift the furnace and where to place it when the charcoal has been kindled and the room warmed. (At an alcove at the back, where it can provide warmth, but where the princess cannot inadvertently touch it and burn herself.)

Another mental check as to when the princess should be coming back tells her it is time for the maids to pour in the bathwater, so she instructs the junior maid to tell the others to do so. She knows the maid is slightly afraid of her, so she accompanies her orders with a smile. This serves only to terrify the girl even more and she bobs her head sharply, then scuttles out of the room.

Bao turns back to the bamboo hamper. What herbs would Her Highness like in her bath tonight? There is sweet grass (*Eupatorium fortunei*), Mulan magnolia and *Osmanthus fragrans*. Bao remembers that the princess once commented that the Mulan magnolia helped her to relax, and a state banquet can be a tiring occasion. That helps the decision. Mulan magnolia and *Osmanthus fragrans* will go into the bathwater.

The girls have fetched two more helpers, yet it is still hard, exhausting work to carry the water from over the furnace and pour it into the bath.

One of the girls complains, 'Why can't we have men doing this for us? They're much stronger!'

Bao overhears and says, 'Are you mad? No male is allowed to enter Her Highness's bedroom and bathroom, ever!'

While the bath is filling Bao lays out a piece of thick hemp fabric on the bricks, and places the princess's personal items on this. There's a bathing towel and bathrobe from the hamper, and a scrubbing implement of volcanic rock. The princess has a few pumices, all made of pretty stones and carved with beautiful geometric patterns. She might not use the pumice, her skin having been carefully pampered and smoothed before the banquet, but Bao is sure that the princess would like to play with it during her bath.

Abruptly, she notices that next to the bath she has left a *fou* basin and a *hu* bottle specially designed for washing hair. Bao puts these away. The princess won't have time to wash her hair today, and it is not good to go to bed with wet hair anyway. After a moment's thought, Bao returns to the bamboo box and takes out a bronze mirror, which she places next to the hemp cloth.

The bath is just over half-filled, so Bao tells the girls to stop, but to keep the rest of the water warm on the furnace. Perhaps the charcoal burner was not needed after all, for the hot water has made the air steamy. The girls are a bit sweaty, so everyone sits on the floor to enjoy a moment of relaxation before the princess returns home.

An older girl who has been transferred from elsewhere in the palace asks Bao, 'There must be other occasions that are more chaotic than this?'

'Oh, too many! Whenever Her Highness has ceremonial events in her schedule, it always takes a lot of preparation. Last month she attended His Majesty at that ceremony outside the city. You all saw how glorious the princess looked, didn't you? That took a lot of work.'

Bao crosses her arms over her legs and turns to one of the girls who was helping her that day. 'Remember? We woke up at three in the morning and prepared the bath as we have done now. Her Highness stayed in the bath for almost half an hour while she tried different herbs and we washed her hair with boiled cereal water. The early morning was so chilly that we had to put two extra portable furnaces by the bath.

'Then, after the bath, there was a team working on her all at once. One was polishing Her Highness's nails, one holding a bronze mirror, and I was standing behind her combing her hair.

'We couldn't decide between two dresses. First, we tried a darkish purple silk skirt, a long one with a narrow waistline. Then a loose skirt, also long, but with alternative reddish-yellowish patterns. Her Highness chose the second one in the end. That bright red colour looked lovely and cheerful on her.'

Bao takes quiet pride in the fact that she had been in attendance on the princess on that day, and she knows that she had looked rather good as well, despite the fact that she was allowed very little time to prepare herself. She had allowed plenty of time for dressing, but then they had spent hours getting the princess's hair styled just right. The royal hair was too damp for the double chignon they were aiming for, and the whole edifice had collapsed and been repaired twice.

Bao is about to elaborate to the others concerning how she had handled the hair-styling crisis and what hair ornaments she had used. Then she stops, tilts her head and listens, apparently staring right through the walls of the palace. The maids ask if Bao has heard noises from out front indicating that their charge has returned from her banquet. By way of answer, Bao gets up and walks briskly from the room.

Everyone else stands also, and they prepare for the last task of the night.

Incredible bathroom discoveries

The archaeologically excavated Qin- and Han-period bathrooms are of various sizes, and are equipped with different kinds of bathing facilities. The features at the palace in Xianyang are around 40 sq. m and consist of a bath, a well-planned drainage system and heating facilities. The tiled bottom of the bath is connected to ceramic drainage pipes and gutters. A furnace on the wall was used to warm up the bathroom.

Interestingly, bathroom scenes are depicted in many elite tombs of the Han dynasty so as to serve the deceased's hygiene needs in their afterlife. Some bathrooms in mortuary contexts were a realistic imitation of real-life bathrooms. For instance, inside a Han dynasty tomb at the Shiyuan site, one of the side rooms has features dug to resemble a bath and a drainage well. In some other cases, bathrooms were represented through the display of bathing utensils and other objects.

子 SIXTH HOUR OF
THE NIGHT

(23.00–00.00: FIRST PART OF *ZI*)

THE SOLDIER
FIGHTS FOR HIS LIFE

Ma has been in bed for four consecutive days. The medic attached to his troop has only come by twice, each time leaving some pills with the junior soldier who is taking care of Ma. This is not indifference or laziness on the part of the medic, but because the plague has hit the army very hard. Despite heroic work by the military physicians, many soldiers have fallen ill, and because the medics work so closely with the sick, a good proportion of them are now also infected, making the situation even worse. Those medics still on their feet are stretched to their limits through exhaustion, and yet still many patients are left to die unattended.

As a veteran soldier, Ma is fortunate in having a younger soldier who acts as a trustworthy carer to keep a close eye on him, feed him his medicine and make sure that he has water and food (when Ma can keep it down). In the past few years of campaigning, Ma has seen so many people die that he is not fearful of death itself. To a soldier death is commonplace. But if he could choose, Ma would rather die with honour on the battlefield than suffer and die from illness. However, as the plague spreads through the camp, Ma has come to realize that he is not immune.

At the beginning of his illness he felt chills raising goose bumps along the fine hairs of his arms before the cold crept into the joints and then the very bones of his body. The recruit allocated to him as a carer covered him with all the bedclothes he could find and even added some straw to keep Ma warm, but his patient could not stop shivering. With joints trembling and teeth chattering, Ma wondered aloud if his *hun* and *po* spirits were leaving him and death was near.

The same medic who had first diagnosed Ma came back during the second day of the veteran's illness. Even with his experience of the disease, the doctor found it hard to believe that the weakened person lying on the bed before him was Ma. He had sighed with resignation while giving Ma's carer more herbal medicine. 'Yesterday he seemed so vital, so full of vigour, and today he is close to death. Even if he has an iron constitution, he may not win this battle.' The remark was intended only for the young carer, but Ma heard from his bed and replied with a weak voice, 'But, Doctor, I have an iron mind.'

It's not a soldier's place to question his emperor, but as he lies in his cot Ma has time to reflect that the folly of the misdirected and pointless campaigns of Wang Mang are starting to corrode his empire. The Han army has been fighting on the north-east, the west and the north-west frontier, and none of these campaigns has ended well. Under Emperor Wu, the empire's finances were sound and the army was strong. Now Wang Mang's forces are endangered by mismanagement and plague while food and supplies have become scarce even as Wang Mang's ill-considered construction projects keep draining the state treasury.

To these problems have been added political mismanagement and a further debilitating campaign in the south-west. In AD 12, Wang Mang stripped the title of 'King' from Gan, the ruler of Gouding – a branch of the people known as the Xinanyi (Southwest Barbarians). War between the Han and the Xinanyi broke out in AD 14 after Gan was killed by Zhou Qin, the Han governor of the Zangke Prefecture; enraged by the killing, Gan's brother raised his people in rebellion against the Han.

AN EASTERN HAN TOMB RELIEF DEPICTING A BATTLE SCENE WITH
WARRIORS AND CHARIOTS ON A BRIDGE

The Han army marched to do battle on the humid subtropical southern frontier and was first hit by the stubborn resistance of the rebel troops, then struck by diseases endemic to the area. Outbreaks of severe diarrhoea and dehydration ripped through the ranks, followed by the ghastly scourge of a virulent plague. In this remote region, food supplies and medical support have not reached the army in time and thousands of soldiers die from illness or starve to death.

By the time of this ill-fated campaign against the Xinanyi, Ma is already a veteran soldier. Since he joined the army at the age of sixteen, he has come through countless battles relatively unscarred and has also survived some of the most infectious diseases the empire has ever encountered. Only last year (year three of the Tianfeng era, AD 16) his reliably strong constitution eventually overcame a near-fatal infection from yet another outbreak of plague.

Though Ma survived, he was badly weakened by his encounter with disease and was sent home for a long recovery that was as much mental as physical. He always thought of himself as strong, but the horrifying scenes from the plague-stricken camp haunted him throughout his recovery. Every day there were multitudes of people dying and pain-filled screams emanating from the tents. The field outside was strewn with heaps of rotting, bloated corpses left unburied while roving packs of dogs and other scavengers picked at the decaying flesh. It was a living hell.

Yet months of recuperation at home helped Ma to recover his natural strength, and eventually he decided he was ready to rejoin the army in the south. Just this one last campaign, Ma told his wife, and then he was going to leave the army and retire to the village where his family would buy a small plot of land. During his first weeks back on campaign, Ma imagined life on that smallholding, with his sons and their own families living nearby. He would dig a pond and they could keep fish and ducks. As he reached eighty, the court would award him the honour of a cane topped by a carved turtle dove, and, holding this official emblem of respectable seniority, Ma would sit in the sun for the whole morning or afternoon, watching his family go about their business.

Even now, as fate seems determined to derail his plans, Ma clings to his dream and finds in his retirement fantasy the strength to fight the illness. For a while he had seemed to be winning. The fevered shivering of his limbs lessened and he was able to drink water, hold down some thin porridge and, even more important, the liquid containing his herbal medicine. He was over the worst, Ma optimistically assured his young carer. He could now move his arms and legs, the chill was dissipating from his bones, and within a fortnight, he would be back on his feet. Who knows, maybe even sooner – that herbal medicine was wonderful stuff, almost magical in its ability to cure illness. So Ma told the young recruit, though in truth he was trying even harder to convince himself.

It is now the fourth day of his fever, and Ma knows that his earlier optimism was unfounded. Unspeakable pains rack his body, especially his spinal cord. He describes the intense agony to his carer as being like thousands of insects biting and tearing at his bones, but stops when he sees the young recruit getting increasingly panicky. The young man only joined the army a few months ago, and has already discovered that the brutality of military life is nothing like the battle scenes romanticized in paintings. The last thing Ma needs is for his only support to flee, leaving him with no one to assuage his desperate thirst or bathe his throbbing head.

By way of diverting both the lad and himself, Ma starts to tell of how people in his hometown tried to keep disease from their homes. He tells him the stories of the *Fangxiangshi* (square-faced exorcists), and dwells upon their elaborately fearsome appearance. 'He wears a bearskin and he has four golden eyes. He carries a lance and shield to expel malevolent spirits.' Ma brings himself up on his forearms. With his face bathed in sweat and his eyes feverishly bright, he seems to the recruit to be more fearsome than the characters he describes. 'Do you know? I once dressed as *Fangxiangshi* in a *nuo* [exorcism] ceremony a long time ago. I wore the mask and a black garment and was dancing while other people were making noises to intimidate the evil spirits.'

The young carer nods, for he saw such performances when he was a boy, and his father had informed him that the *Shentu* and *Yulei* gods protected people from demons and evil spirits. They dressed as gods of war with weapons and armour. But the carer admits sadly to Ma that his family were too poor to decorate their doors or their home with images of such gods.

THE *SHENTU* AND *YULEI* GODS TAKEN FROM
AN EASTERN HAN STONE-RELIEF TOMB
CARVING IN THE HENAN PROVINCE

Though he is exhausted, Ma cannot sleep, both because of the pain and because if he closes his eyes he fears he might never awaken. To keep the conversation going he asks the young recruit how the lad had come to be in the army in the first place.

It turns out that the young man's father was too ill to serve in the army, and because his other son was too young, the responsibility had fallen on Ma's carer, for all that he had just got married and his wife was expecting their first child. The recruit's face grows melancholy as he describes how his wife could not stop weeping when he was sent away – and that was before they knew he was destined for the savage mountains and broad rivers of the southlands.

It was February when he set off from his hometown, marching south with the army. The recruit described his discomfort as the days steadily became warmer and more humid. After they crossed the river, the scenery and landscape became very different. Instead of the cultivated fields of home, vast stretches of land lay unoccupied, covered with forests or scrub.

As he begins to heat a dose of medicine for his patient, the recruit describes to Ma his wonder at the many different crops in the fields. These southerners are not extremely well-off, but there are not many of them starving either. 'When I saw that, I was thinking to myself that maybe the south would not be as bad as I was imagining. Now I know I only saw the surface, and that the marshes and humidity bring diseases. They tell me that men don't live long in the south, and they are so remote from the capital that when they are hit by disasters, nobody cares enough to rescue them.'

The recruit is getting frantic once more, and so, thinking of the comfort that he draws from his own imagined retirement, Ma tries to steer the conversation in a safer direction. 'What is your family like? Do you have a nice house?'

'We have just built our own home. I helped pave the bricks on the roof. My father said we should build small towers there to resemble the other houses in our family.' The recruit comes from northern Henan Prefecture, which actually neighbours Ma's home prefecture to the west. In an age of great movement, some immigrants choose to stick to old customs as a way of remaining in touch with their origins. The ridge-like roof of the recruit's house has a good view, and from the roof of the new home one can see the ridges of the mountains surrounding the town that his family came from. 'My wife planted trees and flowers this spring in the front of the house. Some of the flowers should be blossoming now,' the recruit adds.

The pot the carer uses to prepare the herbal medicine is boiling, and while the recruit is decanting the mixture into a pot, Ma asks how many doses are left. The recruit says nothing, for the medic had prescribed only five doses, which were to be consumed in three days. Evidently, he believed that Ma would be either dead or on the road to recovery by that time. Neither the recruit nor Ma have been sure whether the medicine was actually helping, but at least it was reassuring when there was something to give him. The carer suddenly realizes the seriousness of the problem, and his immediate concern about what they should do tomorrow is abruptly replaced by the realization that Ma might not actually have a tomorrow.

He has heard the desolate cries coming from a neighbouring tent where one poor soldier has been in a critical condition for days now, and might not make it through the night. Now it appears that his own charge is in a similar condition, so instead of answering Ma's question he tries to distract him by changing the conversation.

'Crossing the mountains on the way here, on one mountaintop it seemed as though the whole world was spread out below me. It made me wonder, where does the ghost go after one dies?' Ma pours the last bit of the herbal medicine into his mouth and ponders the question. The medicine seems to give him a little boost and although the night grows late, his spirits have risen slightly. His carer hesitantly mentions that his grandfather said that ghosts enter heaven through a gate in the Kunlun Mountain, but … the soldier does not know much about this topic so he stammers to a halt.

Ma is too tired to explain that Kunlun is the north-west. It is the central axis of the earth where three mountains form a ladder on which a spirit can climb to the centre of heaven, the northern pole where the God of Heaven and all other immortal spirits live. Even as he thinks this, Ma realizes that his information about Kunlun is also fragmentary. Has anybody living actually been to this distant, fantastic place?

The recruit is talking about the south-west, where the local people say that when a person dies, a gate to heaven, complete with trees and flying animals, appears above the tombstone as spirit and body separate. The *hun* part of the spirit returns to the *tian* (heaven) and the *po* goes into *di* (the earth). The carer stops talking, for Ma's eyes are closed and his body is still.

Ma feels the pain lessen and believes that his aching body has got through the most agonizing stage. The veteran soldier tells himself that he is feeling better, and resolves that when he is fully recovered he will find and climb those legendary Kunlun mountains. 'I will fulfil that dream one day,' he vows with his last coherent thought as his consciousness slips away.

Plague outbreaks

There were at least seventeen severe outbreaks of plague during the Western Han, almost half of which occurred in military camps during campaigns. Mortality was particularly high in the camps due to the concentrated population and the soldiers' weakened immune systems during military operations. The plagues took place after natural disasters such as earthquakes and floods and although systems of disaster relief and medical help were established very early by the central government, none were ever adequate.

Conclusion

From these twenty-four stories, we have had a glimpse of twenty-four ordinary characters in one hour of their lives. This one hour is really just a snapshot of their normally hectic, laborious and prolonged working days. Nonetheless, from that hour, we know how the farmer was practising the new *Daitianfa* (rotational farming) to produce more crops while also growing worried about the incoming land assessors to register his newly reclaimed land. We know how different craftsmen struggled to adapt to rapidly changing circumstances both in their factories and workshops and from the external pressures of political courts and governing agencies etc. We have seen a small fraction of the relentless work expected of court servants and governmental workers and their constant fear of receiving punishments. Most importantly, we have seen that life was not easy, simple or straightforward for any of them. Rather, it was full of contradictions and while technological innovations and socioeconomic progress brought them many positive changes, their perceptions of their own and their families' future were a mixture of optimistic and pessimistic sentiments. Their acute awareness of the political uncertainty and the precarious natural conditions in which they lived made them more resilient, adaptive and innovative when it came to improving their lives, and prompted them to become ever more devoted to creating an eternal home for their afterlife.

In the Eastern Han period to follow, despite continuously growing tension within and between different sectors of society, that resilience and strong will of the people continued to foster technological innovations and drive economic development. The Han period was a golden age of Chinese history that gave the world many life-changing innovations.

Acknowledgements

The author would like to express his deep gratitude to Dr Philip Matyszak and Gabriella Nemeth. They both spent numerous hours helping the author to reorganize, polish and sharpen the chapters in this book and to make the stories more accessible to the reader. Without their professional help and patience, it would have remained in a much more rough and ready form. The author is also grateful for Dr Charlene Murphy's careful proofreading of the draft of the book.

BIBLIOGRAPHY

Ban Gu, *Book of the Han*, Zhonghua Book Company, Beijing, 1962.

Chen Zhi, *Collection of Essays on the Han Economic History (Lianghan Jingji Shiliao Luncong)*, People's Press of Shaanxi Province, Xi'an, 1980.

Chen Zhi, *Study of the Juyan Han Period Wooden Slips (Juyan Hanjian Yanjiu)*, Tianjin Ancient Books Publishing House, Tianjin, 1986.

Legge, James, *Confucian Analects, The Great Learning & The Doctrine of the Mean*, Dover Publications, New York, 1971.

Legge, James, *The Chinese Classics, Vol. III. The She King; or, The Book of Poetry*, Trübner and Co, London, 1971.

Ma Xin, *Social History of the Rural Area of Han (Lianghan Xiangcun Shehui Shi)*, Qilu Publishing House, Jinan, 1997.

Sima Qian, *Records of the Grand Historian*, Zhonghua Book Company, Beijing 1959.

Sun Ji, *Atlas of Han Material Culture (Handai Wuzhi Wenhua Ziliao Tushuo)*, Cultural Relics Press, Beijing, 1991.

Sun Yirang, *Rites of Zhou*, Zhonghua Book Company, Beijing, 1987.

Wang Zijin, *Ecology and Environment of the Qin-Han Period (Qinhan Shiqi Shengtai Huanjing Yanjiu)*, Peking University Press, Beijing, 2007.

Wang Zijin, *History of Tomb Looting of Ancient China (Zhongguo Daomu Shi)*, Jiuzhou Press, Beijing, 2007.

Yang Aiguo, *Between the Living and the Dead: Study of Han Period Stone-Relief Tombs* (*Youming Liangjie: Jinian Handai Huaxiangshi Yanjiu*), People's Art Press of Shaanxi Province, Xi'an, 2006.

Yang Hong, *The Lost Elegancy* (*Shiqu de Fengyun*), Zhonghua Book Company, Beijing, 2007.

Yang Zhenhong, *Discovered Bamboo and Wooden Slips and Qin-Han Societies* (*Jiandu yu Qinhan Shehui*), Guangxi Normal University Press, Guilin, 2009.

Yu Zhenbo, *Qin-Han Laws and Societies* (*Qinhan Falv yu Shehui*), People's Press of Hunan Province, Changsha, 2000.

In addition, numerous monographs and journal reports also provided fresh and ample evidence from excavations of many important archaeological sites, such as tombs of King Zhongshan, Laoguanshan Han tombs, Mawangdui Han tombs, the Sanyangzhuang site, Yinwan Han tombs, the tomb of Haihun Marquis, the canal remains in Sanmenxia, the Jingshi granary, numerous mural paintings, countless Han stone-relief tombs, cemeteries of convicts, to name just a few.

The author has also benefited tremendously from many studies on agriculture, handicraft production, wine production, lighting materials and lamps, canal transportation, development of medical science, education system, females in Han society, legal and political systems, food and cuisine, religious practices, and many other aspects of Han society. Due to limitations of space, the author is not able to list these authors one by one, but he wants to express his gratitude for these excellent studies.

LIST OF ILLUSTRATIONS

Pages 8–9: Map by David Woodroffe

Pages 29, 96, 198, 222: Illustrations by Aubrey Smith

Page 21: Gold acupuncture needles, Hebei Museum, Shijiazhuang, China. Photo akg-images / Pictures From History

Page 30: Excavation site at the tombs of the Marquis of Haihun State, Nanchang, Jiangxi, China. Photo Xinhua / Alamy

Page 36: Book on obstetrics, unearthed in 1973 from Han Tomb 3 at Mawangdui, Changsha, China. Photo © Hunan Museum, China / www.hnmuseum.com

Page 46: Polychrome terracotta horses, Shaanxi, China. Private collection. Photo akg-images / François Guenet

Page 51: The Golden Horse of Maoling on display at Shaanxi History Museum, Xi'an, China. Photo © depositphotos

Page 57: Pottery agricultural model, tomb artefact. Photo Granger Historical Picture Archive / Alamy

Page 65: Scene from the Wu family shrine, Shandong, China. Photo The Picture Art Collection / Alamy

Page 70: Bronze TLV *Boju* mirror with Four Spirits and Companions. Photo Sepia Times / Universal Images Group / Getty Images

Page 80: Pottery boat, Guangzhou City Museum, China. Photo Hbcs0084 / Dreamstime.com

Page 90: Inkstone unearthed in 1978 at Jinqueshan, Linyi, Shandong, China. Photo BabelStone / Wikimedia Commons / CC BY-SA 3.0

Page 98: Fossilized mulberry leaf cast, Sanyangzhuang, Henan, China. Photo © Tristram R. Kidder, Washington University in St. Louis

Page 107: Tomb panel, Eastern Han Dynasty; Rogers Fund, 1920 / Metropolitan Museum of Art, New York

Page 117: Brick relief with salt-mining scene, unearthed at Yangzishan, Chengdu, Sichuan, China. Photo Werner Forman / Universal Images Group / Getty Images

Page 136: Kizilgah Beacon Tower. Photo CPA Media Pte Ltd./ Alamy

Page 154: Bronze measure unearthed from Chejiguan Han Tomb, Handan, Hebei, China. Photo Shan_shan / Shutterstock.com

Page 158: Silver seal; Charlotte C. and John C. Weber Collection, Gift of Charlotte C. and John C. Weber, 1994 / Metropolitan Museum of Art, New York

Page 169: Tile rubbing depicting hunting and farming. Photo akg-images / Roland and Sabrina Michaud

Page 186: Clay brick, Xianyang Municipal Museum, Shaanxi, China. Photo akg-images / Laurent Lecat

Page 206: Stone horse outside the tomb of General Huo Qubing near Xi'an, Shaanxi, China. Photo Panorama Media / agefotostock.com

Page 211: Tomb of Emperor Jingdi, Han Yang Ling Mausoleum, Xi'an, Shaanxi, China. Photo Gary Todd / Flickr / Public Domain

Page 230: Female pottery dancer, tomb artefact; Charlotte C. and John C. Weber Collection, Gift of Charlotte C. and John C. Weber, 1992 / Metropolitan Museum of Art, New York

Page 234: Two terracotta vases decorated with acrobats, Western Han period, Musée Cernuschi, Paris, France. Photo Guillaume Jacquet / Wikimedia Commons / Public Domain

Page 241: Bronze lamp with wild goose catching fish, National Museum of China, Beijing. Photo Rowanwindwhistler/Wikimedia Commons / CC BY-SA 3.0

Page 243: Bronze incense burner, Western Han Dynasty; Severance and Greta Millikin Purchase Fund / Cleveland Museum of Art, Cleveland, Ohio, USA

Page 250: Rubbing of tomb brick relief. Photo Werner Forman / Universal Images Group / Getty Images

Page 253: The gods *Shentu* and *Yulei*, stone-relief tomb carving. Public Domain

INDEX

Page numbers in *italic* refer to illustrations and captions.